S0-AFS-977

Legal
Beagle

Legal
Beagle

Diary of a Canine Counselor

Linda A. Cawley, Esq.

New Horizon Press

Far Hills, NJ

Copyright © 1996 by Linda A. Cawley, Esq.

All rights reserved. No part of this book may be reproduced or
transmitted in any form whatsoever, including electronic,
mechanical, or any information storage or retrieval, except as may
be expressly permitted in the 1976 Copyright Act or in writing
from the publisher.

Requests for permission should be addressed to:
New Horizon Press
P.O. Box 669
Far Hills, NJ 07931

Cawley, Linda A.
        Legal Beagle: Diary of a Canine Counselor.

Library of Congress Catalog Card Number: 96-68928

ISBN: 0-88282-146-6

New Horizon Press

Manufactured in the U.S.A.

2000 1999 1998 1997 1996 / 5 4 3 2 1

Legal Beagle is dedicated to
my wonderful husband, Jerry Burden;
my son, Jack, who is the greatest spirit of my life;
and all of the dogs that have shared our lives—
Penny, Tara, Dar, Anke, and Tucker.

A talking bird was the only eyewitness to the murder of his owner. He constantly repeated:
"No, Robert. Robert, no."
Robert was the name of the ex-boyfriend of the woman, and he was charged with the murder. . . .

Acknowledgments

Thanks to the attorneys and support staff in my office and others who have helped develop the concept of dog law.

Thanks to the experts who, through their testimony, allow dog law trials to succeed: animal behaviorists, veterinarians, animal control officers, groomers, breeders, and handlers.

And especially thanks to all of the dog owners who have pursued justice on behalf of their pets. Without their perseverance, there would be no dog laws.

Finally, a special thanks to Artie Hayden and her Beagle, Lucky, who is featured on the cover.

Author's Note

These are my actual experiences and history, and this book reflects my opinion of the past, present, and future. The personalities, events, actions, and conversations portrayed within the story have been reconstructed from my memory and research, utilizing court documents, press accounts, and the memories of participants. In an effort to safeguard the privacy of certain individuals, I have changed their names, and in some cases, altered otherwise identifying characteristics and locations. Events involving the characters happened as described.

Contents

Prologue

I sat in front of the austere, mahogany-paneled court-room listening to the judge read my clients the riot act.

"I do not appreciate your bringing this action into my courtroom. I," his sonorous voice rose and paused, "I have child abuse cases, and rape cases, and murder cases waiting to be heard, and you—" Here he lingered over the word and stared straight at me. "You," he repeated, his voice now with a steel edge, "are fighting over a dog."

As if on cue:

My huge, thirty-five-pound, black and white furry client, whose leash its owner held, began to bark.

My tiny, black and white puppy client, imprisoned in his crate, started whimpering pitifully.

My human client began to cry.

The attorney for the opposition jumped to his feet, overturning his chair, and loudly began to defend his clients' ludicrous position.

Amid the uproar the judge's gavel crashed down.

"Order in the courtroom," the judge yelled, banging his gavel again. "If that puppy isn't turned over immediately, someone here is going to jail." His eyes glowered.

The scene was out of control. I covered my head with my hands and laid it on the table in front of me for a moment trying to regain my sanity. One thought careened through my mind. *How in the world did I get here?*

1

Penny, the
Tricolored Hurricane

It is my earliest memory. At little more than two years old, I was standing clutching the bars of my crib crying when my oldest brother, Eddie, who was nine, came rushing into my room. He grabbed me in the most awkward of grips, bear hugging me from behind. Wobbling down the long hallway leading from the bedrooms, we made our way to the kitchen. I was sure I was going to fall, but was so preoccupied with the journey on which we had embarked I forgot to cry. In the kitchen my freckle-faced cousin Tom waited. He was much older than I, at least thirteen. Tom joined us in our trek towards the garage.

No one else was home. It was the first weekend in May of 1963. My brother Tom had made his first communion that morning and the rest of the family were at the church. Eddie and my cousin had been left behind to baby-sit. Upon arriving at the back door of the house which led to the garage, Tom swung it open at the same time that Eddie set me down on the ground. Suddenly coming at me full speed was a ball of fur, a streak of browns, whites and blacks. I screamed, turned, and ran as fast as my little legs would carry me into the family room where I climbed on top of my father's chair. The fluff ball was tight on my heels. As she stood on her hind legs yapping at me, I tottered precariously on the back of the armchair, sure that any second I would fall into the jaws of death. Such was my first encounter with my first dog. Strangely enough with that unlikely encounter my love and dedication to dogs began.

Penny was a tricolored collie. Later I was told she wasn't show quality because the white ruff around her neck was not complete, and her tail had too much curl. But she was the best pet and companion dog of which any child could have dreamed. And though my two older brothers claimed her also, I always thought of Penny as my partner in life. When I learned to say my prayers at night, I ended them, "God bless Mommy and Daddy, Tommy and Eddie, and Linda and Penny."

Wherever we went, Penny went too. We were insepa-rable. Our house in Cleveland, Ohio was next to the local country club. Each winter the golf course turned into a sled riding area. We dragged our sled nearly a mile into the course to the hole with the steepest hill. There we built a fire and spent the afternoon riding our sleds down the three tiers of the course to the creek below. Barking all the time, Penny exu-berantly ran along side each of us as we made our way both up and down the hill. At the end of such days, the ice and snow compacted in her paws, and she had to stop every so often to chew the ice off, which only made matters worse as they soon froze again. When we finally made it home, Mom towel dried us and Penny too. After all, she just wanted to be one of the gang, and she was.

Penny never minded the snow no matter how bad the ice, but water was another matter. In the summertime, my friends Jayna and Sheila Wagner and I liked to go to Lake Erie where we swam and played in the waves. No matter how far out in the water we went Penny stayed on the shore barking for us to come back. But nothing could get her into the water. One day we walked the length of the Rocky River Pier and jumped off to see if Penny would follow us. She kept whimpering and trotting to the water's edge but she wouldn't jump in. Finally we swam out far away from the pier and suddenly she came running off the end of the pier, landing in the water with a splash, fighting to keep her head from getting wet. She raced with us back to shore, but never went near the water again. As much as she wanted to be with us, it wasn't worth the agony of getting wet.

Not long afterward we took Penny to the veterinarian to be groomed. Playing with us in the woods, she had gotten sticky burs throughout her coat. My mother told the veterinarian to "trim" Penny's coat and get the burs out. Instead he shaved her. She came home looking like a greyhound. I tried to tell her she still looked wonderful to me but she was so embarrassed by her coat that she wouldn't go outside. For weeks she sulked. Even though I instructed all of the neighbor kids not to laugh at her, she refused to go near anyone. Happily, her fur grew quickly and she was soon back outside with us again.

As much as Penny hated water, she loved cars. In fact, she loved them too much. In the car she always whimpered with excitement as she jumped from side to side and back to front, sticking her head out the windows. The wind made her eyes water. However, if we closed the windows she barked until they were opened again. One time our parents decided to travel by car to a skiing vacation in Michigan. Although I begged to take Penny along, my parents decided to drop her off at the kennel on the way out of town. My brother Tom's friend, John Sweeney, came with us. My parents, the three boys, Penny and I, with all of our equipment piled into the station wagon. As soon as Penny got in the car she started whimpering trying to get to the windows. But the car was so crowded she had to walk across the laps of three boys to get there. Penny weighed nearly seventy pounds so the boys groaned as she pounced from one to the other.

"Does she do this all the time?" John asked, his head buried behind Penny's fur.

"Yeah," my brother Tom answered. "Whenever she gets in the car she whimpers and paces and pounces."

"Do we have to take her?" John asked, obviously picturing a miserable eight-hour drive to Northern Michigan.

Realizing that John thought that Penny was going to travel the entire trip with us, my father, quick to enjoy a good tease, took over the conversation.

"John," he addressed the boy, "now your job on this trip will be to keep Penny happy. She likes to stick her head out the windows so scrunch down and don't worry if she decides you're a seat."

"But I can't even see," the thirteen-year-old said, his voice muffled in seventy pounds of fur.

My brothers joined in my father's joke. "It's not hard," Tom said as he reached over and opened the window. As soon as the window started to open Penny jumped across the three boys to Tom's side of the car. John, who was sitting in the middle, was crunched as she switched directions on him.

Since it was no more than twenty degrees outside the car was soon freezing. Fur flew everywhere and John had Penny's rear end stuck in his face as she pushed her head out the window.

"Mr. Cawley," John said hesitantly, "maybe there's not enough room for me on this trip."

The boys and my father began laughing and clued John in on the fact that Penny would soon be dropped off. I was the only tearful one when we got to the kennel. The others asked if I wanted to stay with her. "We can get a cut rate," Eddie teased. I scowled at him. But I sent Penny postcards as I always did whenever she was away from me.

Penny's nemesis in the neighborhood was "Duke," the dog across the street. Duke was a huge tan, black and gray German shepherd. When we bragged about Penny's feats being as great as Lassie's, the kids across the street countered that Duke's were as great as Rin Tin Tin. It was the era of dog heroes on television.

One day the neighborhood gang was playing out in the field next to our house while I, still too young to take part, was playing in the yard near my father. Suddenly a cry went up.

"Duke got Danny."

"Duke got Danny."

Danny was one of five kids that lived across the field from us. He was also the only really fat kid in the neighborhood. By the time we got there, Danny was on the ground crying, and Duke was nowhere to be seen. Duke had gotten Danny on his fattest part. The kids could not help giggling as Danny got up and ran towards home with his hands hanging onto the torn seat of his pants. However, soon the kids' laughter turned to fear as Duke, looking huger than usual, sauntered towards them.

"Here comes Duke!" one yelled.

Duke, who had been scampering around the neighborhood, had apparently not found anything too exciting. As the kids started to run, so did Duke. Just as he was almost upon us, Duke's owner shouted, "Come here!" The dog turned and headed home while we all breathed sighs of relief. After that, our parents warned us to stay away from Duke.

"He's a German shepherd," my mother said, "and German shepherds are mean and unpredictable."

Despite Duke's tarnishment of the German shepherd's reputation, I soon fell in love with one named Vaughn. Vaughn was the largest German shepherd I had ever seen. He lived in the back room of Michael's liquor store/deli up at the end of the street. Vaughn was actually one of a series of dogs that was left in the store at night to guard the property. They were all named Vaughn. But there was one particular "Vaughn" that I liked best. Whenever we went to the store, I jumped out of the car and ran to the back gate, calling, "Vaughn." He always came lumbering out to see me. And he was so friendly. I was only four, and he was a lot bigger than I was when he was on all fours. My entire hand could fit between his ears, his head was so big. He was my Rin Tin Tin, and also my renewal of confidence in the nobility of the German shepherd.

I visited him as often as I could over the next year or two, but one day when he trotted over I was shocked to see bruises and welts all over his body. His owner told me, "Vaughn was hit by a car in front of the store." I petted Vaughn and held him for a few minutes and then he slowly limped to the back room. A few days later I learned that he had died. Another Vaughn quickly took the job, but he was never the real one to me. I made up my mind right then to some day have a German shepherd of my own.

My best friend during those years was a little boy who lived behind me. He was a year younger than I. Terry and I did everything together. He called me "Yinda." He had five older brothers and sisters, who always considered us the tagalongs. One day, after we had been excluded from whatever adventure the older kids were on, we went over to Duke's house to get one of our playmates.

"I hear them in the backyard," Terry called to me. I followed him around the side of the house. Suddenly he screamed. Duke had bitten Terry in the face.

A few weeks later when we warily went over to Duke's, Penny was at my side for protection, but I didn't need it. I was told that Duke had been "recruited to go to work for the Army." I was impressed.

"I think that the Army will probably suit Duke just fine," I opined with a maturity far beyond my years. It wasn't until many years later that I learned that parents shipped vicious dogs off to the "army" or "police" just as often as unwanted pets got to move "out to a farm."

While I always considered Penny to be one of us kids, my brothers liked to use my love for her to torture me. My cousins had a little white poodle named Chrissie, because she had been born on Christmas. I loved to carry her around and take her to bed with me at night. But my brothers told me that if I paid too much attention to Chrissie, Penny would get jealous and leave us. I never believed them though because I thought of Chrissie as a dog and, as I explained in all seriousness to them, "Penny's our sister."

When I was six, my mother's friend's cat had kittens and since I loved all animals I begged for one. My brothers, my mom and I all drove to the friend's house to pick our cat. The kittens were all black and white except for one gray and white kitty. I chose her and, after great discussion, we decided to name her Tabitha after the daughter on the television show Bewitched. Tabitha loved Penny and went everywhere with her. When we took long walks in the evening, Penny trotted along with us while Tabitha ran from bush to bush and Penny nudged her back on course as we visited playmates around the neighborhood. Sometimes Tabitha crouched on the sofa and waited for Penny to come by. Then she jumped on Penny's back for a free ride.

I developed my friendship with Jayna and Sheila after I started grade school. They were the youngest in a family of seven and spent much time at our house.

Impressed by the concept of adults having jobs, we decided to find people with dogs in the neighborhood who didn't have kids. We asked if we could be their "dog walkers." Many of our neighbors agreed and we would go running off with a new dog to play with, have some fun, and return the dog. We never asked for any money, we just did it out of love. After one of our dog-walking excursions, my father asked the three of us, "So which one of you girls likes dogs the best?"

We each answered, "I do." But I knew that he was as aware as I was that Jayna and Sheila didn't love dogs the way I did. My curiosity and affection for them knew no bounds. By the time I was eight years old, I had learned all of the breeds of dogs listed in the *World Book Encyclopedia*. I knew each one's history and its classification. By then I was sure I wanted to do something with animals when I grew up, but I just wasn't sure what. I didn't like science, so being a veterinarian didn't seem like the profession for me. If I owned a pet store, I wouldn't be able to bring myself to sell the dogs. I read all of the Albert Payson Terhune books the famed author had written about his beloved collies. For a time I dreamed of owning a farm like Terhune's and breeding collies. In the third grade we played *What's My Line?* The contestants had to know more about one subject than the other kids so they could answer questions about their secret careers. To no one's surprise, I was designated the "dog catcher." Dogs, dogs, I dreamed about them and read about them and some day I knew my future work would be with them but what and how and where I didn't know.

One day when I was reading a book about a lawyer who fought for the rights of children I became concerned as to who fought for the rights of animals. I asked my father, "Dad, do animals have rights?"

"Of course they do," he answered as he put down his pen and invited me into his office. I settled in one of the chairs across from my father's desk.

"If they have rights," I questioned him, "why are so many animals put to sleep each year?"

"What have you been reading?" he asked.

I showed him an article from the local newspaper that described in horrid detail the euthanasia of so many animals each year.

"Do you want to do something about this?" He looked seriously but encouragingly at me.

"Yes," I responded. "But what can I do?"

"Here." He reached into one of the many files in his drawers and pulled out a flyer about the American Humane Society and how contributions could be made to save the lives of the many animals destroyed each year. "Here is information about how you can help save animals. Why don't you call them and see what you can do," my father suggested.

I took the flyer and carefully read the information about the needless destruction of so many unwanted animals. I desperately wanted to help save those animals. The following morning I called the number in the flyer and listened to a recording. I was told to send my financial contribution to an address in Washington, D.C. I decided to raise some funds to save the animals.

Once again I employed the assistance of my good friends Jayna and Sheila. Our dog-walking business had grown and some of the people now paid us. We saved every penny. We held carnivals. We sold lemonade, had putt-putt contests, sold Popsicles and everything else we could think of to save the many unwanted pets. Finally we had nearly thirty dollars to send to the Humane Society. My mother agreed to go to the bank and get a check for us. With great relish we sent off the check. We never heard another word. Our disappointment was too great to comprehend. We had worked so hard to save the animals, and yet our contribution received no response. There had to be a better way to help. In the book I had read, the lawyer helped children find homes. I wanted to do that for animals. I knew someone had to help them find homes, and contributing my life's earnings had not been enough. I was determined to learn how to represent the dogs and cats. That's how I settled on my future career—the law. But no one I asked nor anything I read spoke about "dog law." That connection was only in my dreams and the future.

The years passed swiftly. It was a Thursday night in the fall. Our house was located on a half-acre lot in a suburb of Cleveland called Westlake. The street was a dead end and had little traffic. One block over, however, was Hilliard Boulevard, a four-lane road divided by a median. Once you crossed Hilliard, suburbia disappeared and you were immersed in thick woods and azure ponds.

For some reason we never learned, Penny developed a desire to travel into those woods. Every chance she got to run off, she headed there. Neighbors on Hilliard were always calling to tell us, "Your dog is on her way into the woods again." Each time, my parents issued the order "Go and get her." I could never do it. I pictured her getting hit by a car as she was coming back to me. I couldn't bear the thought of seeing her hurt, so I would go in the opposite direction to search for her. Sometimes I cried because I was so scared of finding her dead. This made me angry that she had gotten out in the first place. We never had a fence in our yard, no one did. There were no leash laws then either. We had a run for Penny but she was only in it when no one was in the yard with her. But most of the time she played with us and quickly learned how to escape from sight right in front of our eyes. She would involve us in play and while we pretended to chase her she would scamper away and then return for more. Once she knew she had us hooked on the game she would run around the side of the house and take off for the woods.

One night when I was about sixteen I was watching television in my room when the unthinkable happened. My mother called me and I went out to the kitchen where my father stood putting on a jacket, not looking at me. I knew right away something was wrong.

"We think Penny's been hit by a car," my mother finally said.

I was stunned. "How did she get out?" I asked. I don't think I could have said it in a more accusing way.

My father turned to me and replied, "I had her outside with me. I was putting out the garbage and she ran off." As he walked out the door, he turned towards me and his voice broke. I had never seen my father so emotional before. "She just gets away from us. You know how she likes to go to the woods."

"Is she dead?" I had to ask.

"We think so," my mother sadly answered. "She was hit in the head as she started to cross Hilliard to come home. It was a hit and run. Dad's going to get her now."

I started to cry. I was angry that Penny had gotten out. I was angry that someone had killed her and wasn't going to be punished. It was then I think I made up my mind somehow, some way I would right the wrongs done to animals. I would be their champion.

When I met friends years later they said it was then I began to speak of being a lawyer although how I would bring together my love of animals and the law was only a distant dream.

I still have Penny's collar with her tags on it. And I still cherish a portrait of her that shows her imperfect white ruff that got her classified as a pet puppy and brought her into our home. But most of all I have all my memories of her spirit. My love for dogs and my joy in their companionship came because of my bond to Penny. Her death was the greatest loss I had suffered and hers was the greatest love I had yet known. Penny's death so affected me that, for years, I could not talk about her or of getting another dog without crying. I was upset that we had been so foolish to allow her to run free. But I came to realize it was her running free that had made her our best friend.

When I was finally ready to love another dog, it was almost time for me to go away to college. My parents were insistent that another dog didn't make any sense because I would be leaving home soon, and they didn't want the obligations of a dog. But I begged and begged for a collie, a breed on which I'd set my heart, but my parents held their ground. Unless I could take the dog with me, I couldn't have one. So I started my campaign to find a solution and to overcome the obstacles.

First, I had to find a college that would accept me and the dog. I started by writing a letter to every college I might possibly consider attending, from Minnesota to Florida, from California to New York. It was a lengthy and tedious job. There were no word processors available. But I was determined.

Dear Admissions Department:
I am a sophomore at Magnificat High School in Rocky River, Ohio, where I maintain a 4.0 grade average. I am in search of a college that will allow pets on campus.
Sincerely,
Linda Cawley

I received many responses. Some told me to get rid of my dog. Some counseled me to leave my dog at home. Some lectured me on the inanity of picking a college based on whether they allowed pets.

My most favorable and most sympathetic response came from the University of Colorado in Boulder. They assured me that they would work something out if I chose their school. That was all I needed for ammunition with my parents. I could take my dog to college with me. Now all I had to do was find the right dog.

Though I wanted another Penny, my parents felt collies were too big and needed too much care because of their long fur. So I decided to look for the next best thing, a little Penny—a Border collie.

While traveling in Ireland a few years before, we had visited my father's uncle who lived on a farm. He had sheep, cattle and, of course, Border collies. One day while we were at his farm he asked if we would like to see his dog work. We all responded enthusiastically. "Not only does the dog have to retrieve the sheep from all over the surrounding land but he has to pick out my sheep from the other sheep which share the grazing land," Dad's uncle explained. He gave his dog a quick command. The dog scampered off into the underbrush. He quickly cut out the proper sheep and herded them back to the farm. We were all astounded and impressed.

Then Uncle Michael gave his dog another command. The dog reacted differently this time. He lowered his head and moved a few paces away from my uncle. Then he stopped and looked back. My uncle repeated the command. The dog moved a few more inches and looked back. Uncle Michael said to us, "He thinks I'm daft. It's not time to get the cattle." The confused dog was released from the command and allowed to rest in the farmhouse. An hour or so later he got up on his own and headed out to retrieve the cattle, according to schedule.

Border collies were relatively new to the United States in 1976 and not too easy to locate. But through Dog World

Magazine I found a breeder in Ohio, John Holgate. One weekend my parents and I drove out to his farm to see the dogs. Holgate showed us a working exhibition of his dogs cutting sheep and obeying a variety of commands for herding exhibitions. Once again we were impressed by the skill and intelligence of Border collies. A litter was due that summer and we reserved a puppy. I anxiously awaited the new arrival. On the Fourth of July we went back to the farm to pick up our bicentennial puppy.

Tara's temperament took a little getting used to. She was a herding dog. She was bred to work. I soon found that a bored working dog will find other activities. Tara certainly did. She took it upon herself to retrieve anything in sight, in the hopes of someone throwing it to her. When you weren't in the mood for a game of fetch, she pestered you and began a game of her own. She retrieved objects of all sizes, pieces of paper, matchbooks, anything she could find. She was also afraid of the World. Despite as much socialization as I knew how to give her, she became a fear biter, without the ability to ever inflict a bite.

Even taking her to obedience class was a problem because she was so skittish.

Although she obeyed perfectly, the class, taught by a husband and wife team, had a requirement prior to graduation in which the dogs had to stand still while the instructor came around and petted them. I knew Tara would not put up with that. The instructor knew that she would not put up with it. "I'm going to refuse to touch her," the husband said.

Remembering that Tara tolerated women better than men, I asked, "What about your wife?"

He agreed. I watched when he told her. The wife looked like her husband had just sold her to the sharks. She approached Tara cautiously and gently placed a hand on her head. Although the dogs were supposed to stand still during this exercise, I could see that Tara was relaxing at the touch of the woman, so I didn't reprimand her when she jumped up on the woman's arm in a friendly manner seeking personal contact. They passed her despite the fact that the rules were slightly bent. And no one got bit.

I think Tara's fear of men was acquired, and not so irrationally, from her introduction to my brothers. Tom and Eddie had been traveling across the United States by van during that summer. When they returned home they had long hair, half beards and ragged clothes. They thought they looked cool. Obviously, Tara thought they had just arrived from the moon. She took one look at them, ran, and hid behind a table. Instead of backing off, my wonderfully obnoxious brothers began to chase after the puppy, confirming her fears. In reply, she peed on the floor, snarled, and hated men from then on.

I wanted to train Tara for obedience work, but her exuberant, excitable temperament made me discard that notion. She quickly became a pet, and soon it was time to head off to college.

2

On the Road

The summer after my freshman year my parents decided to allow me to take their car back to school with me since I would be living off campus for my sophomore year. Tara and I started out on my first cross-country trip alone. About halfway across Indiana it started to rain. It was soon raining so hard I could barely see the road in front of me. I pulled off the road for a few minutes to look around but there was no place of refuge in sight. I was surrounded by farmland. When the rain began to let up a little, I started down a country road in search of a gas station or other place to stop. As I was driving along I suddenly noticed the sky turning yellow; then, right in our path, a funnel cloud loomed ahead. Quickly I pulled the car off the road into a ditch. Telling Tara to lie down on the floor of the front seat, I got down on top of her to protect her. The dark cloud whirled around, heading straight for us. I don't know who was more scared, Tara or me. But the tornado finally passed by and we moved on down the road and towards my future.

When Tara and I arrived at our new apartment, I couldn't wait to introduce her to my roommates.

"Tricia! Jill!" I shouted into the three-bedroom house we had rented for the school year. "We're here!

"It's so great to be back," I exclaimed as we all hugged each other and they greeted Tara.

Our rental house was on the bike trail to the University of Colorado campus. I had an old bike we called "beater bike." It was one speed and had a coaster brake. I had bought it at a used bike store the semester before. When I asked the seller if this was the kind of bike I would need to lock up, he told me that all I had to do with this bike was rope it and no one would take it. It was perfect for a college campus.

Soon after classes began, I led Tara into the back of the auditorium for my economics class. The auditorium seated about 150 students. Tara lay at my feet quietly during the entire lecture. Then suddenly everyone stood up to exit the room and Tara jumped up and started barking wildly. I grabbed her and tried to make a quick departure, but not soon enough. Everyone had noticed the dog in the classroom.

After that incident, I decided to train Tara to stay outside and wait for me. She was great at heeling to the bike. She would stop at every intersection and obey my hand signals from the bike for slowing down and sitting when necessary. I decided to start her slowly with the waiting outside. I would park the bike, put Tara in a sit-stay and enter the building. I would watch from behind the glass doors. She always stayed perfectly. Soon I felt comfortable leaving her for extended periods of time.

One time I left her outside the student union while I ran in to sign up for the next semester's classes. I was delayed longer than expected and when I returned nearly twenty minutes later I found Tara at the automatic teller machine retrieving things for people to throw for her. She had paper cups, an old glove, a tin can and other assorted garbage. I apologized to the people in line for the machine but they had enjoyed her act.

"Come on, Tara," I called to her, and off on the bike we rode. We soon became a familiar sight all over campus, even though everyone knew Tara as the dog who retrieved garbage.

My senior year of college I moved into a house with a woman who loved dogs. The three of us hiked the mountains and camped in the wilderness. Tara loved the outdoors and loved running free. The entire time she was in Boulder I don't think she was ever on a leash. But I never feared for her safety because she had been trained on how to cross streets and how to wait for me at my bike. She was a wonderful companion and went everywhere that I went.

I even took her to the campus radio station where I had a radio show each week. She rested at my feet while I was on the air. I dreamed of working after graduation in a radio station where I could take my dog with me to work. I hunted for a radio job at every station in Colorado, but without success.

Finally, shortly after graduation, I received a call from the program director of a new radio station in Vail, Colorado. Although I was only offered a few weekend hours on a part-time basis, I felt I had to take the job to get started in radio. I soon found a weekday job selling tennis shoes at a sporting goods shop. I found out that, in Vail, even working two jobs I could barely afford an efficiency apartment. Despite exhausting my options, there was no way I could take the job in Vail and live there with Tara. It wouldn't be fair to her, a dog that liked to run and work, nor to me and my budding career. So I placed the following ad in the *Boulder Camera*: "Help! I cannot commit my dog to a life of condominiums. Have to move, need good home for six-year-old Border collie."

I was fortunate to receive a response from an older couple looking for an older Border collie. It was a wonderful match even though it tore my heart out to have to "give away" my dog. I cried for days. She was gone and, despite knowing that I had done what was best for Tara, I felt more alone than I ever had since Penny died. I swore to myself I would be sure to wait until the perfect time for a dog before I opened my heart to another one.

I only spent a year in Vail. I worked as a disc jockey, a newscaster for a radio station, and later as a news producer for a television station in Aspen and Vail. Although I loved Aspen and still do, I hated Vail. I felt trapped and stifled. There was not enough intellectual stimulation, even though I loved the rush of adrenalin I received from working in radio and television.

It was the end of my second summer in Vail, after a great season of playing unlimited golf on the wonderful courses that grace the Vail Valley, when it suddenly hit me that I was about to enter another "off-season" in the mountains. The spring off-season had featured tremendous mud slides. I had been trapped in the Vail Valley by a snow storm as late as June of that year and I wasn't ready for another rainy season. I panicked.

Suddenly, one night in late August of 1984, it hit me that I had to go to law school. The following Friday was my next day off. I drove to Boulder and asked when the deadline for admission to law school was.

I was told, "Last March."

"March?" I questioned. "But doesn't school start now?"

"The deadline was March for the fall semester."

"But I want to enroll for this fall."

The clerk looked at me like I was crazy. I went to the records department and picked up a copy of my transcripts.

Then I took my transcripts and headed for the main campus of the University of Denver and the College of Law. I was told that the law school was located on a different campus. Not being too familiar with the city, I didn't know where anything was. I drove out near Stapleton Airport to what used to be Colorado Women's College which I had been told was now the University of Denver College of Law. There I found a beautiful campus, sixty acres covered with grand Gothic buildings, with a modern law school in the center. I loved the campus and immediately knew that I wanted to attend the law school no matter what.

At the admissions office I was told that classes for first-year students had already started, but if I filled out an application and could supply my LSAT scores, I might be able to fill the seat of a no-show.

I drove back to Vail and spent the evening completing my law school application. My LSAT scores had been very good, but my grade point average was rather low. When I had applied to universities for undergraduate study, I had applied to a few Ivy League schools. The applications for those schools required essays, so I was familiar with what admissions boards were looking for. I wrote an essay explaining why I wanted to get into law school and, most important, why I wanted to get into law school TODAY! I had been reading Ayn Rand's *Atlas Shrugged*, so in my letter I wrote: "No man is more depraved than the man without a goal. My goal is to go to law school and fight for animals' rights. I have delayed one year in that goal and to delay another would only serve to delay the goals of my life."

Two days later I received a call while I was doing the news on the morning show at the radio station, telling me that I had been accepted and that I would have to be at classes the following Tuesday evening. I would have to attend night school until I caught up with the day division classes. Within three days, I quit my job, moved to Denver and began getting ready for law school. I couldn't wait.

3

The Search for the Perfect Career and The Perfect Dog

As soon as I started law school I knew I had made the right choice. I wanted to study hard at law school and to go on and fight for the rights of animals. But how I was going to combine the two I wasn't quite sure.

While I worked at the radio station, I saw firsthand how crucial a good FCC attorney was to a broadcaster. The station had problems with issues of ownership, frequency designation, transmitter location, and program content issues, all of which required legal advice. I was frustrated by the legalities which seemed to hinder the growth and development of the fledgling station, but I kind of liked the world of media, though it was far from the picture of an advocate fighting for the rights of animals which I'd held in my mind since childhood.

In my third year of law school I was lucky enough to be selected for an internship with the National Association of

Broadcasters in Washington, D.C. However, by the time I graduated the FCC had deregulated broadcasting and there was not much demand for FCC or Communications Law. So when I returned to Colorado to finish my last year of law school I still hadn't found an area to specialize in.

Soon enough the semester came to an end and graduation took place. I sent out resumes to nearly every law firm in the Denver-Boulder area, but job prospects did not look good in the summer of 1987. The only fields of law that were hiring were bankruptcy and divorce. I didn't want anything to do with them. They sounded boring and depressing.

A couple of weeks after graduation I flew out to San Diego. While sitting in a hotel room on the Coast Boulevard south of La Jolla, I picked up a local telephone book and looked under the "Attorney" heading. As I was idly looking at the specialities, I noticed an attorney whose name seemed to pop up under many of the subheadings. His name was Paul C. Prentiss. So I called him.

"I'd like to speak to Mr. Prentiss, please."

"Hold one moment."

"Paul Prentiss," a musical baritone announced into the telephone.

I gathered my nerve. "I discovered your name prominently displayed in the attorney listing in the phone book and I want to move to California after taking the Colorado bar exam next month."

He laughed. "I believe in multiplicity of choice," he said.

"Me too," I said.

He seemed to like my spirit. "I taught at the University of Denver and might be looking for a clerk this fall," he said. He set a time for an appointment. Then he added, "I know that every law student has one good suit, and I don't want to see yours, so just wear whatever you are comfortable in."

Considering that my usual attire was jeans, this was very inviting. I was trying to avoid stuffy law firms, and his certainly didn't sound stuffy. At the appointment I appeared in jeans, as did he. As I later learned, the instructions were for his benefit, not mine, because he was always in jeans unless a client came into the office.

I began working for him and learned quickly to appreciate his vitality. He wrote law articles and books on art, copyrights and trademarks; he gave lectures to literary clubs, art associations, and other interested groups. Often I would accompany him on these expeditions.

One day I mentioned to Paul the possibility of trying to find a field of law that suited me. Paul was the master of marketing a boutique law firm. He was renowned for his work in art law, and he also specialized in entertainment law, literary law, education law, and copyrights and trademarks. It was from Paul that I learned that any specialty of law can precede the word law to create a marketable field. It was also from Paul that I learned that the best kind of specialty is one which emphasizes what you feel passionately about. Paul loved art, music and literary properties.

"What do you love?" he asked me that day.

I didn't have to think about it.

"Dogs." I smiled. "And they don't have the money to hire me to fight for them."

"They don't," he smiled back, "but their masters do."

"But no one has ever practiced dog law."

"Well then, you have a wide-open field," he said. "No competition."

From then on my mind percolated on the possibility.

Always in the back of my mind was my desire to get another dog. The time was never right. Either I was moving around or lived in a place that didn't allow them. Now I decided I wanted to wait no longer. I had not had a dog since Tara, so this was going to be a major step. This time I wanted to be sure to get a dog that was the "perfect match" for me and I for him. First, I had to find a place to live that allowed pets. I had been living in a condominium near the ocean, but with a dog I would need a yard. A yard in La Jolla was a sign of wealth. I didn't have wealth. So I began my search for a beach cottage. One day while riding my bike around the Wind and Sea area of La Jolla I saw a For Rent sign on a six-foot wooden fence. I followed the fence around the corner trying to see into the yard, but the fence continued all along the property line. I leaned the bike up along the fence and stood up trying to see into the yard.

A voice from behind the fence said, "Can we help you?" I nearly fell off the bike with surprise. I saw the tenants staring back at me.

"Yes, I'm looking for a house to rent."

They welcomed me in to see the place. It was a one-room cottage, with only one closet in the whole house. But it was surrounded by the large yard. In fact there was probably twice as much yard as house, and, better yet, it was fully fenced and allowed pets. I rented the cottage. I could move in on October 15. Since it was only August 15, this gave me plenty of time to find the dog of my dreams.

So the search was on.

I researched buying a dog the same way I research every other issue in my life. I bought a book: *The Right Dog for You.* I figured this was the best place to start. I wanted to determine which breed would be right for me. Since my days of memorizing dog entries in the *World Book Encyclopedia* a lot of new breeds had come on the scene.

I knew I wanted a large dog, a medium to long coated dog. And I was sure I wanted a working breed dog. I always was and still am dedicated to herding and working dogs. But what makes a selection difficult is that I am fond of just about every breed of herding and working dog!

However, since I lived alone and traveled by car throughout California, I decided I wanted a protection dog. I considered a variety of breeds:

Collie: A classic dog, but not much in the field of protection. I don't think a collie would ever attack to protect its owner. At least not to the degree I felt necessary.

Leonberger: A grand large dog that looked like a lion, hence its name. A rare breed, but after inquiring at the national club I was lucky enough to find a breeder who had recently moved to La Jolla and, better yet, had recently bred a litter of pups. I went to visit. The pups were little bears, huge and cuddly. The mother was protective and smart. But she was just too big for a beach cottage. I needed a dog that could live peaceably in the back of a car or in a hotel room and yet guard my small house.

Kuvasz: a Kuvasz breeder lived about fifty miles east of San Diego. One weekend I drove out to see the dogs. The puppies looked like little lambs. They were all identical with little black eyes and black noses, otherwise all white. But when I went out to see the adult dogs, all I saw was fur. White fur blew across the kennel, across the yard, across the fields, across the highway, and everywhere. There was too much fur, and it was all white.

Bernese mountain dog: A very attractive tricolor dog that was also protective. But I was afraid it might become too "one-personed," and I needed a dog that was adaptable and personable. It was also very big. I drove up to Big Bear California to visit a breeder there. When I saw the beautiful mountains that the dogs lived in, I saw why they were called mountain dogs. It suited them. I didn't think they would like beach front living without winters.

German shepherd: Another classic. Protective, intelligent, sociable, large but not too large, long haired but not too long haired, but hard to select because there were so many of them, German or American, working or pets, long coats or short, black or white, large boned or standard, Schutzhund or AKC.

I was drawn to the shepherd but since my only experiences with German shepherds had been Duke, the tyrant of my childhood, and Vaughn, the dog who'd been trained to ward off intruders, two completely different dogs, how could I be assured of getting a puppy with the friendly temperament I wanted?

Once I had read all I could find about the German shepherd, I began making the rounds of dog shows and breeders. The dogs at the dog shows were pretty, but not the friendly shepherds I was looking for. I wanted a large square German shepherd with a thick coat, and big-headed like Vaughn. I began looking for working dogs. I went to training sessions and saw some incredible dogs. The dogs would attack the agitator aggressively and then run over and jump in someone's lap to be petted. The dogs were incredible. I fell in love. And now I knew what I wanted.

While searching, I also began to think about my conversation with Paul about dog law. Each breeder I talked to sent me home with information about their breed lines, and a contract. Being a lawyer, I probably read the contracts more closely than most buyers, but I didn't find one that I felt would be legally binding. More important, I didn't think the contracts would do what the breeders believed they would do, and they didn't protect the buyer either.

By now I had passed the California bar exam and was practicing law with Paul as an associate. I enjoyed art and entertainment law but I remembered the passion we'd spoken of. I was not passionate about his specialites the way Paul was. I knew I could be passionate about dog law. I wasn't sure though that Paul would permit me to take dog-related cases in a firm that marketed itself as an entertainment law firm. I outlined my idea for him that dog law, which was initially named canine and equine law, could come under the umbrella of entertainment law, because show dogs and racehorses were a form of entertainment. He nodded and I knew I'd won. The next issue to be addressed was how to attract clients. There was no listing for Dog Lawyers in the yellow pages. I wanted to put an ad under Pets but Paul didn't think there would be enough business to cover the cost of the ad. "You'll have to pay it so check out the market." I decided to talk to the breeders I was meeting while looking for a dog.

Labor Day weekend of 1988 was rapidly approaching. I was going to drive up to Big Bear for the final weekend of the summer. I was going alone and wished I had my new dog to go with me. My dog would love Big Bear, I was sure. I looked forward to the lake and the mountains, the horseback riding, and boating. One of the breeders I needed to see lived on the way. I scheduled a stop to see her puppies. Kate Baron was a young woman with long blond hair. Three small children were playing in the yard and she held a baby while she talked to me. Her husband, Dennis, was rounding up the puppies from the backyard.

The healthy looking rambunctious puppies were about three months old, which was surprising. I had read that it's not preferred to leave Schutzhund bred pups with the parents past eight or nine weeks of age. The pups need that month to develop their own self-confidence, not to be treated like the little sibling or the mother's pet. But the pups were all active and friendly. One really caught my eye. His name was Ben. He came over to me and laid his head on my feet while I talked with Kate and Dennis.

"Do you have a contract for the sale of your dogs?" I asked.

"No," Dennis answered. "We're not professional breeders. We just sell them to the buyers we like."

"I'm an attorney," I explained, "and I'm thinking of starting a practice for dog owners. If you could have a contract drafted by an attorney for a reasonable price, would you?"

"Sure," Kate piped in. "We've had trouble before with people returning puppies or claiming they were entitled to refunds when there was nothing wrong with the dogs. But we have always been afraid of contracts because we were afraid we might put something in there that would get us in trouble. However, we need to sell these puppies now as they're getting past the best age to have them leave."

"Here's my card," I said as I handed them one of my newly prepared dog law cards. "Let me know if I can do anything for you. But I don't think I can take Ben right now. I think it would be better to wait until I'm settled in my new home before I take a dog. Since he needs a home now, I'd better pass." As much as I wanted a dog to accompany me to Big Bear, the timing wasn't quite right. All my emotions said yes, but logic prevailed, and I went on to Big Bear alone. A few weeks later I went to see a Schutzhund practice.

There were a variety of breeds there, including Dobermans and Rottweilers, but most of the dogs were German shepherds. The training took place on the grounds of the Schneider Kennel, run by Gail Burton. I watched with amazement as the dogs went through their attack work. One dog, a black shepherd named Siegfried, caught my eye. After attacking the agitator with such force that I thought for sure he would be injured, the dog was given a command and ran back to the chair where his owner was sitting, as friendly as a puppy. He was goofy too. He tried to climb in my lap for some petting. But when Gail called him, it was back to the attack work. I instantly fell in love with Siegfried and learned he was a three-year-old Schutzhund III male, who was one of the kennel's stud dogs. But none of his puppies were going to be available for the next four months. I would be moving into my new house in October and really didn't want to wait until January for the puppy. It was finally the right time for the dog, and I wanted him now. I told Gail that I was practicing dog law, and she immediately hired me to redraft her contracts and liability waivers for the Schutzhund practice that took place on her property. I now had my first dog law client, and Paul now saw that people were willing to pay for the service.

While I was mulling over whether to wait or find another dog, I saw an ad in the paper for Schutzhund puppies. I called. I learned that the female was owned by a breeder named Sally Stein and, surprisingly, the female, Greta, had been bred to Siegfried. The same Siegfried I had fallen in love with. Her pups would be ready for new homes in six weeks. I had to see them.

That weekend I went to see the pups. There were four males in a litter of nine. One was pitch black and reminded me of Siegfried, but he was feisty. He was the Green puppy, so identified by the color of his collar. At that point I selected him. But there were two other males, Yellow and White, who looked alike and were the largest of the litter. They were calmer than Green but not as black. I'd wait and see.

In the meantime I had received Paul's permission to advertise canine and equine law in the San Diego yellow pages so long as I paid the costs. I agreed. The problem was that there wasn't a category for animal law. The other fields didn't make sense, so I elected to put the ad under Dog Services.

Two weeks later I went back to visit the pups. They were now four weeks old and full of energy. And they had personalities. Yellow and White were the most outgoing and dominant, and the fattest. Green had developed into a testy little guy, and too ornery. The fourth male pup was too small and too timid for me. It was down to Yellow and White. I watched them play and saw them explore the grounds.

Then Sally, who had been watching, said, "You can choose either one, but I do have a lady who has requested the yellow puppy."

I figured that was serendipity. How could I take a puppy that someone else had set her heart on? If I chose that dog and it got killed or sick, I would always blame it on the fact that it was not supposed to be my dog. My dog would be the one with the white collar. Sally agreed and told me to return in six weeks.

After I finished preparing the contracts for Kate and Gail, no new clients popped up. The yellow pages had come out, but no one seemed to notice the dog lawyer advertised under Dogs. Or maybe no one had need of a dog lawyer. I was disappointed, but decided to do some self promotion. I talked to the dog clubs around town, and the breeders I had met had given me their business cards so I sent them announcements about my new practice, but still no dog clients. I was starting to get concerned that I might never be able to pay the cost of the yellow page advertisement, no less combine my love of dogs and the law.

Thanksgiving weekend was coming up and this was the week I was supposed to get Dar, my new puppy. He was to be named after Dar Robinson, the stunt man in the movie *Lethal Weapon.*

On the Wednesday before Thanksgiving, I left work about six to go get Dar. "He's beautiful!" I exclaimed when Sally brought him into the room. I could hardly believe the pup I had watched grow since he was two weeks old had turned into this perfectly proportioned, handsome little dog. We completed the paperwork, including the typical breeder contract which guaranteed Dar against hip dysplasia so long as he was x-rayed at one year of age and diagnosed by then. Acting as my own attorney, I negotiated a provision that would permit me to keep the puppy even if I became entitled to a replacement dog because of a hereditary problem with this puppy. I knew myself well enough to know whatever the reason I could never give him up. I signed the contract and took the puppy.

Because I had to go back to the office to complete my work I took Dar with me. He curled up in the back of my chair while I researched some law cases. That was, he slept when he wasn't kibitzing with the other employees by nipping at skirts, chasing feet and shredding scrap paper. But like me everyone was charmed by him.

He must have brought me luck too, because when I returned to the office on Monday morning there was a message from a reporter for the San Diego Union. He wanted to interview me about my practice of dog law. He had seen the ad in the yellow pages and was curious. Returning his call, I described my intended specialty and told him about my life-long love of animals. The article ran in the Sunday edition. The following morning the phones were ringing off the hook. Dog law had begun.

4

California, Where All Things, Including Dog Law, Begin

From the deluge of phone calls I received after the Union article ran, I had to select the cases I could best handle. One call came from Leigh Johnson who had left a message that she had purchased a dog from an importer and the dog was not what it had been represented to be. Because fraud can be a serious claim, I immediately returned her call.

Leigh told me what had happened.

A breeder, Lorraine Deutsh, who also imported dogs from Germany, had sold a rotweiler puppy to Leigh and her husband, Gerry, representing that the dog was a Schutzhund (ScH) II and therefore worth five thousand dollars. The dog came with a scorebook which showed her scores, qualifying her to be a Schutzhund II. After a few training sessions with their new dog, whom they named Marcella, it became apparent that Marcella was not of champion stock and may not have even been a Schutzhund at all. She didn't even understand basic obedience commands. The Johnsons began to investigate. They soon learned that the signature on their dog's paperwork had been forged. They demanded a refund. Lorraine Deutsh refused. They brought the case to me and I demanded a refund. Deutsh still refused, insisting that Marcella was a Schutzhund dog. We filed suit.

I felt that Deutsh not only had breached a contract but, by misrepresenting the dog's qualifications, the importer may also have committed fraud. Deutsh had represented that Marcella had qualifications she didn't have and which, in my opinion, Deutsh must have known she didn't have. The sale of goods, which dogs are considered, based upon any misrepresentation of a material fact such as the dog's qualifications, constitutes deceptive trade practices for which the buyer may be able to recover treble damages.

In order for a dog to get points for a Schutzhund title, it has to go through a competition in which a score is awarded by the judge. In this case, the dog had supposedly obtained her Schutzhund title in Germany. The scorebook indicated three competitions in Germany where the dog had received her points. After having the scorebook translated to English, I contacted the agency which had sponsored the events and learned that the judge whose "signature" was on the scorebook had not even been in attendance at the events cited. It appeared that the importer had forged signatures on the scorebook. I had the handwriting analyzed by a forensic expert who compared it to Deutsh's signature on court documents. Although we were never sure whether it was an exact match, the importer agreed to settle by compensating the Johnsons with another dog.

Another call soon came in also as a result of the Union article. "I'm Jill Beckett. I live in Las Vegas. A friend called me after reading the article about you. I breed Shar-Peis."

I must have sounded vague about my knowledge of this breed because Mrs. Beckett explained, "You know, the dog who looks like a wrinkled rug."

The image clicked. I knew because of their sudden popularity breeders were turning out litter after litter to cash in and were selling them often at very high prices. "Go on," I said.

"Well," she said. "I sold a prize puppy pursuant to a co-ownership agreement in which the buyers agreed to show the dog until it obtained a championship. I would retain breeding rights."

"That sounds all right," I mused.

In an excited throaty voice Mrs. Beckett continued. "Well, I want my little boy returned. There is a lot of money in it for you." This comment gave me my first grounds for suspicion but I let her continue. "I had a contract with the buyers of the puppy and they are in breach."

"I will need to see your contract to determine your rights," I told her.

Her voice turned indignant. "Well, I know what my rights are. My husband is a graduate of Yale Law School and he drafted the contract for me."

"Then why don't you have your husband enforce it for you?" I questioned her.

"Well," she stumbled, "we want you."

Actually, I think she just wanted me to hear her story so in the event the other party to the contract called me I would have a conflict of interest and could not represent them. Regardless, I was intrigued and wanted to know more.

"I will need you to send a copy of the contract," I repeated. "Then I can tell you whether I will take your case."

Now her tone was haughty. "My husband is a Yale Law School graduate and he says I have the right to recover the dog and one hundred thousand dollars. I just want you to call them and get me my dog and the money," she persisted.

I couldn't imagine what was in the contract that had led this woman to believe that she was entitled to recover a hundred thousand dollars from the buyer of the dog, but I couldn't wait to find out. If dogs were really worth that much money, there might be a living in dog law yet, I figured.

"I'm sorry, Ma'am. Unless you send me the contract there is nothing I can do for you," I told her politely.

"If I send it to you, you have to promise me that you won't copy it for use with other clients. My husband is a graduate of the Yale Law School," she repeated for the umpteenth time, "and the contract is quite extensive and we can't have you using it for other clients."

"I promise I won't copy your contract." How could it benefit my other clients if it had got her into this dispute? She said she would get back to me.

Apparently she did not get her dog back because about a month later I received the contract. It was a sale/co-ownership agreement that was single spaced, front and back of no fewer than ten pages. The wording and legal clauses were overwhelming. I was an attorney, and I didn't have the patience to read the contract. But I pushed myself to pore over the document, highlighting the pertinent provisions. Unfortunately, as I soon learned, anything pertinent also appeared to be unenforceable. The "Yale Law School" graduate (I never did learn whether he ever practiced law) had so painstakingly drafted a contract overwhelmingly in favor of his wife and to the unconscionable detriment of the buyers of the dog that he had defeated his purpose. He had created a legal document that was unenforceable, at least to such an extent that she would ever get one hundred thousand dollars or the dog.

As in that case, sometimes a contract can be too strong. In drafting a contract each side needs to negotiate fairly in order for the contract to form the clear understanding of the parties. If one party cannot understand the contract, is not represented by counsel, and the dominant party drafted the contract, it will be construed against that party, and may not be enforceable against the naive party, if they never really understood what it was they were agreeing to in the first place. A contract is a "meeting of the minds." If the minds never meet, then there is no contract. If there is no contract, the courts try to put the parties back where they were before they entered into the agreement. This is called rescission of the contract. But rescission is not always the best option when an animal is at issue. If the dog has been owned since puppyhood by one party, who would stand to lose the dog in a rescission action, the court will not cause an unconscionable result to occur.

The Yale Law School grad had included a provision in the contract for liquidated damages. When it is difficult to establish what the monetary damages would be to one party if the other were to breach the agreement, then liquidated damages (a set amount) can be agreed to in a contract. This contract provided that for every breach of the contract (a contract which included at least one hundred requirements for what the buyers had to do to comply), they would be assessed ten thousand dollars in damages. According to the breeder, the buyers had breached the agreement at least ten times, and therefore owed them one hundred thousand dollars. I refused to take the woman's case because I didn't feel it would be fair to enforce such a burdensome contract on an unwitting buyer. I chalked all my research up to a learning experience. I was still learning the pros and cons of dog law. I soon realized I would have to be very selective in choosing my cases and to have reputable clients acting in good faith in asserting their claims before my new specialty would gain any respect. If I succeeded, not only would I have opened up a new area of law but my childhood dream of fighting for the rights of animals would be fulfilled.

The first dog law case in which I felt that I truly helped someone who needed my help was also my first "dangerous dog" case. At that time, a dog in San Diego County was deemed dangerous if it had bitten or attacked twice within two years. One sunny June day I received a tearful call from Helen Forrester who told me, "My son has been charged with owning a dangerous dog. They want to put the dog to sleep. Can you help us?"

I agreed to meet with Helen and her son, Ron, in my office the following day. "Bring the dog, Skipper, with you," I told them. After all, he was going to be my client too and I needed to judge his temperament.

Helen Forrester, a sixty-five-year-old woman dressed in a much laundered blue skirt and blouse, and her son, Ron, entered my office. Ron, dressed in overalls, was in his forties. He was handicapped and lived at home. The dog, Skipper, was a black Labrador mix with a long silky coat. He calmly walked into the office and lay down next to Ron.

Skipper was Ron's pet. They'd been together since Skipper was a puppy. Mrs. Forrester and her son did not appear to have much money, but they had a lot of love for their dog, and for each other. I wanted to help them. They were terrified that they might lose the dog.

Ron began telling me what had happened. He spoke with a heavy stutter so it took a long time.

"Skipper was tied in the front yard while I worked on a car parked in front of the house. Mom's dog, Ralph, another black Lab mix, was also tied out front. The neighborhood children and their parents had been told on numerous occasions not to run through our yard and not to go near the dogs."

"They did it anyhow," Helen interjected.

She picked up the story and the pace.

"Some neighbor kids, Kristy Bolan and Ben Haber, who lived on each side of our home, were playing together. They came up the driveway unattended. Kristy started petting Skipper's head. Ben came up from behind, and Skipper turned and nipped him."

"Because two bites are required," I told them, "I need to know about the facts surrounding the dog's first biting incident."

Surprisingly, I found out it was the same little boy who had been bitten. But then he had only been two years old.

"The first incident occurred," Ron said, "when two-year-old Ben came on our property with his father who was holding his hand. We had Skipper tied up. Ben walked up to the dog. Neither his father nor I, with whom he was speaking, saw him, and the little boy tried to remove a bone from Skipper's mouth. Well, you know how animals are about their food. Skipper bit him."

I nodded. "The issue though, Ron, is whether a two-year-old is capable of provoking the dog by taking the bone away. I'll argue that he provoked the dog which, if successful, would eliminate the first bite. But because Ben was only two years old I'm afraid he was too young to be legally able to provoke a dog. Let me think about it."

Over the next few weeks I did some heavy thinking and research and finally came up with a backup defense: The Dog Lineup.

The "trial" was to take place at San Diego Animal Control offices. An animal control officer would be acting as judge and the arresting officer as prosecutor. As the defense counsel, I could call witnesses and cross-examine their witnesses. The key witness would be Ben, the boy who had been bitten.

I obtained photographs from the Forresters of Skipper and Ralph and added a few other black dogs as well. At the hearing I approached Ben, a boisterous six-year-old. "Can you select the dog which bit you?" I asked, knowing the incidents had occurred when he was four and two years old. Ben fingered first one photo then another. I could see by the puzzled look on his face he was unsure. Finally he made a selection.

"That's not Skipper," I announced and argued the mix-identification of the dog. "The dogs all look enough alike that Ben is unable to tell which one had bitten him on which occasion."

The judge, nee animal control officer, nodded.

"Either way," I continued, "it can't be proven which one of the dogs was the biter. Therefore Skipper should be permitted to return home."

I scrutinized the judge's face. He was blinking his eyes and looked like he agreed. I think the animal control officer serving as judge appreciated the lengths the Forresters had gone to defend their dog and had given them some leeway.

"Not guilty," he ruled. "Skipper can return home."

I felt energized by my win. This time I'd done it. I'd saved a dog from destruction and salvaged his home. It was going to be fun creating defenses for dogs. I couldn't wait for the next case I could take to trial.

Shortly after this, I received a call to appear on the local television station on their morning news program. I took Dar with me and on *Sunup San Diego* told stories about dogs and the law. After the show I received a call from a harried sounding woman, Ethel Gordon.

Ethel was insistent on needing to meet with me immediately. "I have to talk to you. That S.O.B. killed my dog," she shouted into the phone.

"Who killed your dog?" I interrupted her, trying to get some facts.

"That S.O.B. did. I told him he was killing Chief but he didn't care."

I still had no information as to why she was so upset, but I could tell she was too distraught to answer questions. I would have to let her tell her story her way.

"My dog, Chief, was my best friend," she sobbed. "Everybody will tell you that we went everywhere together. And that S.O.B. killed him."

"Who?" I jumped in.

"Dr. Dembry at Central Animal Hospital."

"Ethel," I said. "I want to help you but you're just not giving me the information I need."

After pulling teeth to get relevant information out of Ethel I had what I believed to be a clear-cut case but, as I soon learned, no dog law case is clear-cut. Ethel had a golden retriever named Chief. She was elderly, on welfare, and Chief had gone everywhere with her, from collecting cans to her medical appointments. But one day Chief had become lethargic.

"I took him to my usual veterinary clinic, but instead of seeing our usual vet Chief was seen by Dr. Dembry. He told me to take Chief home to rest," she said.

She paused, and I could hear her sniffling.

"Why don't you get yourself a drink of water, Ethel, and then come back.

"Then what happened?" I pressed when she returned to the phone.

"Well, I took Chief home but he only got worse. He quit drinking water. So I took him back to the vet. He put Chief on insulin for diabetes."

She was sobbing again so I waited. "Ethel, can you go on?" I asked.

She murmured, "Yes" and continued. "I took Chief home and gave him the insulin as instructed. He went into convulsions that night and died."

I felt sympathy for this poor old woman who had been robbed of her only friend, perhaps needlessly. I took the case and had the medical records pulled from Dr. Dembry's office and reviewed by a veterinarian who could serve as an expert witness, Dr. Kehane. Dr. Kehane called to say he would testify that if Chief had been diagnosed with diabetes on the first day he had been brought to the veterinary clinic he would have survived, but because his condition had so degenerated by the time he received the insulin, it had been too late and he had died. We filed suit for veterinary malpractice against Dr. Dembry and the veterinary clinic.

At the deposition, Dr. Dembry, a thirtyish dark haired man with an air of smug confidence, denied doing anything wrong, even though he was no longer practicing veterinary medicine. The insurance company for the veterinary clinic was unwilling to settle. We had no choice but to take the case to trial. It would be my first test of a dog law case in the California courts.

I felt I had developed all of the right arguments. "The dog died," I said solemnly, "because of Dr. Dembry's 'failure to diagnose.' If the dog had been treated properly from the beginning, Ethel would not have suffered her loss.

"The damages were great," I continued, "because Chief died as a result of Dr. Dembry's reckless disregard for the dog's life, for which, under California statutes, punitive damages are recoverable."

In addition, I argued the dog had "peculiar and sentimental value. I believe California case law will support recovery for the emotional distress suffered by Ethel Gordon in losing her beloved pet dog, Chief."

Chuck Weingard, the attorney for Dembry and the clinic, argued, "The death of the dog didn't cause your client emotional distress. She had already been distressed prior to the loss of the dog by other factors in her life."

When claiming emotional distress damages, a person's entire emotional life becomes open to examination. Ethel had quite a difficult history. I didn't want her to suffer more at trial. I moved for a settlement. The defense wouldn't budge.

Next, the defense filed a motion to dismiss. They claimed that Ethel suffered from emotional problems prior to Chief's death and therefore suffered no damages because the dog had no value. The motion was set for a hearing.

At the hearing I prepared for every argument. I had photos of the dog. Ethel was dressed in her one fancy outfit and prepared to testify. I had psychological records showing the great loss suffered by Ethel in losing Chief. I had Dr. Kehane's expert opinion as to the cause of death and the negligence committed by Dr. Dembry. I had written medical opinions as to the ability of a dog to recover and survive if diabetes is diagnosed and treated promptly. I had neighbors testifying about the close relationship between Chief and Ethel. Everyone was present in the courtroom when the bailiff announced, "Will the Municipal Court for the County of San Diego please come to order."

Everyone stood as Judge Monahan entered the courtroom and took the bench.

"Attorneys in the *Gordon vs. Dembry et al* case, please approach the bench," the judge began.

I approached the bench along with Dr. Dembry's attorney. Judge Monahan, a sixtyish man with a tan and gray hair brushed back from his face, looked more like a tennis pro than a judge. But the glare in his eyes showed that he was upset and very serious in what he was about to say.

"Ms. Cawley," the judge addressed me, glaring down from the bench. "Are you serious about this claim?"

"Of course, Your Honor," I responded, surprised by his challenge.

"This is a dead dog case, Ms. Cawley," the judge stated as though that explained everything.

"But, Your Honor," I began in an attempt to defend my position. He interrupted me.

"I will not have a dead dog case in my courtroom. Motion to dismiss granted."

Legal Beagle

The judge's decisive dismissal definitely took the wind out of my sails. Now I had to tell Ethel, who had so excitedly awaited her day in court, that she would never get to speak, that her case had been dismissed without argument. Not only had she lost her pet, but now she had no recourse. She could not afford an appeal so the case would be closed. It was so unfair. It reminded me of my question to my father so long before, "Don't animals have rights?" He had assured me they had but I had seen creatures robbed of them so often I was beginning to doubt it.

This made me realize I had to figure out how to present dog law cases so that they would be taken seriously. I knew that owners really suffer distress when they lose their dogs, but the law would not support legal action to recover damages, even though California had both statues and case law that appeared to permit such cases.

The next wrongful death case to come to me was from Minneapolis, Minnesota. The Hudsons, a young working couple, had owned two red chows, Mika and Red. The dogs had been secured in a backyard surrounded by a six-foot wooden fence while the Hudsons were at work. On the day at issue, Mika and Red had apparently escaped from the fence by crawling under. They were discovered running free by animal control. Two officers in an animal control truck then proceeded to chase the dogs across town. The dogs ran and, according to the report, the truck chased them for five miles. According to the autopsy, however, Red's pads were worn down as though he had run many more miles than five.

The dogs had run back to their home. They ducked under the fence and escaped animal control by getting back into their yard, or so they thought. One of the officers was overheard by a neighbor yelling at the dogs, "I'm going to get you now, you so-and-so dogs."

As the neighbor described it, "He was arguing with the dogs."

The officer then climbed over the fence with a restraining stick and was later seen by the neighbor pulling Mika back up and over the fence with the stick. The dog was dragged by the neck out to the truck and tossed into the back. At the time Mika was placed in the truck he appeared limp to the witnessing neighbor. The officer then went back into the yard, captured Red, and dragged him back over the fence by his throat. He too was tossed in the back of the truck. At that point there was blood all over the sidewalk and in the truck. The officer asked to use the neighbor's hose to wash down the blood from the sidewalk and out of the truck. A note was left on the Hudsons' front door telling them where to find their dogs.

The Hudsons arrived home that afternoon and went immediately to animal control. Red had already died. Mika was lying in the kennel, still suffering from major injuries about the head and throat. He could not walk because of cut and torn pads on his paws. He had not been treated by a veterinarian. The Hudsons became hysterical. They requested medical treatment for their dog and were told that none was available until they paid to have the dog released. They immediately paid the impound fee and took Mika to their own veterinarian. Mika survived with medical treatment, but the Hudsons wanted to take legal action against animal control.

Now I was faced with another wrongful death case, but at least it was out of California in a new jurisdiction and we would have a different judge. I would try again. I compiled the evidence against the officers. I had an eyewitness who had seen and heard everything. I had medical records to indicate the severity of the injuries to Mika, and an autopsy to establish that Red had died as a result of strangulation. What I hadn't prepared for was the defense of governmental immunity, the one they used.

Because animal control was operated by the county which was a governmental entity and because the government is immune from committing negligence, the county and its animal control officers could not be held liable for their "negligent" treatment of the dog.

I could argue that the officer had acted outside the scope of his employment, but because restraining dogs at large was his employment, he hadn't. I could argue that he acted intentionally in injuring/killing the dogs rather than negligently, but then my only defendant would be the officer, not the county. The difficulties of governmental immunity when dealing with dog cases have since become a major complication in all wrongful death and malpractice cases. Animal control officers, police officers, and state university veterinarians may all be immune from negligence causing injury or death to an animal, as outrageous as the negligence may have been. To proceed on the Hudsons' behalf against the government would be prohibitively expensive. The Hudsons dropped the case. Another wrongful death case had gone unrighted.

My frustration with dog law grew more intense. How could people and animals suffer these injuries only to be told that they had no legal recourse? I now knew that the clients' likelihood of success in court was very low and the expense of litigation could be very high. It wasn't fair.

By now I had been practicing dog law for two years. The level of my own frustration fighting dog laws in the legal system had now reached a peak. I couldn't seem to help a lot of the aggrieved owners who came to me needing counsel and assistance. When I tried even harder, I only got more discouraged fighting the legal system. At the lowest point I'd been since I'd begun combining my dreams, I packed my two German shepherds, Dar and Anke, who I'd recently acquired, into my Chevy Blazer and took off on a cross-country trip to figure out what, if anything, I could do about animal rights and the law.

5

On the Road Again

With no plans as to where we would go or what we would do, and little money, we hit the road and headed north out of San Diego.

The first night was Easter Sunday. Dar was one-and-a-half years old and Anke had only been with us four months. She still was distrustful of Dar although he constantly fawned over her. I just hoped they didn't fight all the way across the country. Outside of Yosemite National Park I found a Motel 6 that allowed pets. It only cost $12.99. What I didn't count on was who else would stay in a motel where they allowed pets and only charged $12.99 on Easter Sunday. All night long cops banged on doors and announced their presence. Loud domestic disputes, bottle-breaking drunken brawls, raucous drug busts, and assorted and sundry other crimes complete with sound effects punctuated the dark. I put Dar out in the Blazer to guard our things. I kept Anke inside with me. None of us got much sleep.

The next day we started into Yosemite National Park. My spirits were lifted by the rushing waterfalls, tall pine trees, and snowcapped peaks towering over blue lakes. I thought the dogs would enjoy exploring the woods. I hadn't counted on them hating the winding two lane road. We had to stop every couple of miles to let them run off energy. Up on a peak looking like it was suspended in blue sky, we found snow. Dar had never seen it before. He went crazy running his nose through it and rolling in it. Nearby was a gully with a rustic log bridge. Feeling adventurous, I started to walk across the log and Dar followed. Being still a pup, he thought he could do anything I could do. He followed me until we were over the gully which lay six feet below us, and then he froze. Lying down on his belly, he began to whimper like a baby. I ran to the other side to show him how. Anke, without hesitation, ran down the gully, through the ditch, and up the other side, something that didn't occur to Dar. But now he couldn't go back and he wouldn't come forward. Walking back on the log, I tried to help guide him but he wouldn't budge. How could I move a hundred-pound German shepherd across a two-foot wide log? I couldn't. I went back across and waited with Anke.

Letting out a big yelp, Dar jumped up and with two leaps covered the distance of the log, jumping across the gully to join us. Going back, they both ran through the gully. Dar was learning.

I drove north through Merced and Fresno and then headed east towards Reno, Nevada. We stopped halfway over the mountains in a town called Placerville. The next day we drove toward South Lake Tahoe. We stopped and played in the woods along a stream and at the lake with its ice blue water. It was great to see the country from a dog's perspective.

After camping out overnight because I couldn't find a motel, we headed for Nevada, since I had decided I wanted to take the bar examination for that state. In Reno we stayed at another Motel 6. I was becoming fond of them since they always allowed dogs. Since all Motel 6s had the same floor plan, the dogs knew right away where their water and food would be and where each of them would sleep. The consistency of the rooms gave them some consistency in their lives.

Looking around, I thought the area would be a great place to live. It was similar to Colorado with its mountains and skiing and yet Reno was sunny year round. But spending a couple of days there with my dogs, I learned that Reno was probably not the best place for us. I met a young woman who was a model for Coors beer. She had a cute puppy with her that loved to play with Dar and Anke.

"You don't want to live here," she told me.

"Why not?" I asked. "It's beautiful."

"The men," she answered. "If you ever want to marry don't live here. The men don't treat women too well. And in business they hate women."

After a few days of further observation I came to understand what she meant. Nevada was still the Old West. Women attorneys were not favored, and I could see it would be tough starting a dog law practice in Nevada. I decided northern California might be a better bet, and so we packed up and headed west to the San Francisco area. Arriving in Los Gatos, I stumbled on another problem. Nothing was cheap, and no place allowed dogs. We finally gave up and spent the night in the truck. Anke slept in the front seats while Dar and I shared the back. Both my clothes and I were sprinkled with fur. The next day we stopped in a Laundromat to clean up and then traveled through San Francisco and north into Napa Valley. Clouds made the coast area overcast so we crossed over the valley eastbound to Interstate 5 and then north into Oregon. We toured the impressive redwoods hundreds of feet high and the beautiful University of Oregon in Eugene, but just as I was thinking maybe this was the place for us, we got stuck in Portland in the worst rainstorm I'd ever been through. The rain and hail pelting us was difficult on the dogs and me, so we traveled east again. Along the Columbia River we viewed with awe the sea-sculpted scenery, caves, towering arches, and natural and manmade bridges and finally came to the Windsurfing Capital of the World, Dalles, Oregon. The only visible motel was on a hill overlooking the valley.

"Do you allow pets?" I asked.

"What kind of pets?"

"Dog," I answered, intentionally leaving the s off dog.

"We do as long as it's well-behaved."

"Oh, very well-behaved. And very well-traveled," I added, still not letting on that there were two of them and they were German shepherds.

"I suppose it will be okay. But we have cats and we don't want them chasing our cats."

"No problem," I promised, and there wasn't.

After relaxing at Dalles we headed north through Washington and over to Seattle. Not knowing where our next destination was, I saw a ferry port. I drove up and asked when the next ferry would be leaving and where it was headed.

"Victoria," was the crusty old-timer's curt reply.

"How long?" I asked, paring my own words down.

"Tomorrow."

"Tomorrow? Where is that ferry going?" I asked, pointing to a large ship sitting in the harbor and gearing up its engines.

"Orcas Island."

"When does it leave?"

"Right now."

"We'll take it."

I had no idea where or what Orcas Island was, but I thought it would be a good change of pace. By this time I'd formulated a list of two things that I wished dogs could do when traveling: 1) Help with the driving, and 2) Take photographs. All of the pictures from the trip were of the dogs. Finally, on the ferry, I got someone to take a picture of us sailing across the harbor.

Orcas Island was an animal lover's paradise. I rented a cabin. Dar and Anke ran free outside. Right in front of the cabin, sea lions—the largest of which weighed two thousand pounds or more—played in the water. Anke only watched while Dar exuberantly chased after them up and down the shoreline. We hiked the craggy mountains on the island and stayed until the weekend when we were kicked out because the weekend tourists from Seattle were coming over. That Friday morning we caught the once-a-day ferry to Victoria, British Columbia.

In Victoria I was amazed to find out that Butchart Gardens, the one-hundred-thirty-acre Borchart estate, permitted dogs on the property. Of course, I don't think they ever thought two German shepherds would be coming and surveying up close the seven hundred varieties of flowers.

After taking the ferry back to the mainland, I found a motel north of Vancouver that had been listed in the AAA book as permitting dogs. After I signed in, the clerk at the desk looked out the window and saw the two massive shepherds staring back at her from the Blazer windows.

"Are those your dogs?"

"Yes," I admitted.

"Well, they can't stay here."

"But it says in the book that you allow dogs."

"We do," she answered, "but not those dogs."

After that I learned to park the car out of sight while checking into motels, even if pets were allowed. After viewing the tall fir trees and mountains which seemed close enough to touch in Vancouver, we traveled through Glacier National Park to Banff. In Banff we found a park filled with hundreds of friendly elk. The big animals grazed the verdant fields or they quietly rested next to me while I sat on a picnic bench. The dogs didn't move an inch, but only watched in fascination. Later, we saw them grazing on the town common undisturbed by humans or domestic animals.

Many national parks do not permit dogs. I always feel, this is unfair. Dogs seem to be closer to the wildlife than people. Well-trained dogs can be quite an enjoyment when exploring. We traveled south through Yellowstone, and the dogs got a close-up look at buffalo, elk and deer. In Wyoming we got stuck by a flock of sheep being herded down the road. Whenever we could get close to wildlife, I would speak very softly and calmly to the dogs. They learned to stay calm themselves. From Yellowstone we traveled south through the middle of Wyoming and Colorado to Aspen.

Legal Beagle

In Aspen we discovered a fox's den while walking through the fields along Roaring Fork River. There were three darling kits that were no more than six weeks old. The dogs approached the den, and the kits came out and teased them playfully. They all stared at each other without fear. Even the mother did not appear threatened by the dogs. Animals seem to know when they are among friends. Each morning for the week we were in Aspen we visited with the fox family. Then one day we came to the den and it was all roped off. Some wildlife preservation society had discovered the den and they were going to "protect" the animals by roping them off and standing guard over them. They wouldn't even let the dogs walk on the trail anymore, yet they felt it was all right to have a person stand there watching the mother and her kittens. A few days later, the mother moved her family farther into the wilderness. Sometimes animal rights organizations try to "do good" and do too good. Naturally wild animals, in my opinion, should be left alone in their own habitat. If others want to see them, human and animal, they can tread there not disturbing the environment. The animals will decide who is their friend and who is not.

By now we'd traveled more than eight thousand miles in six weeks. I wanted to get back into dog law. I was reenergized. Dog owners needed someone to advocate their rights and, difficult as it had been in California, I wanted to search for answers. I drove from Aspen to Denver where I had gone to law school, and it was there I decided I could open a practice. Colorado didn't have so many laws against dogs. Also, with Denver's central location, I could work with dog issues in all of the states. I began to search for a place to live.

Touring rental homes, though, was discouraging. Owners took one look at me and my dogs and said, "No thanks." No one would rent to an unemployed single woman from California with two German shepherds. Knowing that my landlord from California, Jenny Singer, lived in Denver, I looked up her address in the telephone directory and stopped by to ask if she would give me a letter of recommendation so I could rent a house in Denver.

"We have a house here for you," Jenny said.

"Where?" I asked.

"Washington Park," she answered.

"I'll take it," I told her, sight unseen. She insisted I see it first so we immediately went out to the house. "It's perfect," I said. It had a big fenced-in yard for the dogs. Within a month, I was moved into the new house in Denver and setting up my dog law practice once again.

This time, the uniqueness of my specialty and the whole concept of dog owners' rights which was new to Colorado drew people's attention and they began to call before I'd even opened my office. When I did, the media fastened onto me since my first case was a dog alleged to have committed a murder.

6

America's Most Wanted

The body of ten-year-old Tim Taylor had been discovered alongside a country road about a half mile from his home. Tim had last been seen at 9:00 p.m. the evening before when he had been put to bed by his mother. The mother had left at about 1:00 a.m. to deliver newspapers. According to his testimony, the father had been at home sleeping, and a baby was also in the house asleep. The boy and his father slept in the same room. He was discovered at 9:00 a.m. on a Friday morning. He had been dead for at least seven hours. After the autopsy, the coroner listed the cause of death as "exposure."

According to police, Tim had apparently left the house to chase after his mother's departing car. She had not seen him following her and had driven off. Hearing the boy's cries, my client's dog had allegedly broken free from his chain, escaped over a fence and attacked Tim as he was running down the road. The dog was found on its owner's front porch the following morning with blood on his paws. The dog was impounded that day and destroyed.

My clients, Teri and Dick Ryder, were a working couple with two children themselves. The parents and their two kids, a daughter, Sara, fourteen, and a son Sam, ten, came to me in tears. They lived nearby in a town named Corella. The population of Corella was less than five thousand. The entire community was upset and shocked at the death of a child. Dick, the dog's owner, had been charged with the crime. But he had been sleeping in his own bed as he did every night. His dog, an Alaskan malamute named Telly, was thought to be secured in the backyard. "And here I am," Dick explained, "faced with possible jail time."

The family could not have been more upset. They had had an attorney but when they learned that I specialized in dog law they came to see me pleading for help.

Because I had never handled a criminal defense in which the defendant could go to jail if he were found guilty, I decided I needed to consult with a cocounsel who had criminal defense experience. An attorney I knew, Harry Hopkin, was noted for his criminal defense work. Harry agreed to join me in a consultation with the Ryders. After they'd explained their story, Harry shook his head and said, "They want to put you in jail."

The whole family burst into tears. I felt I had to search for some hope for them.

"But don't they have a good defense in that they did not act negligently, and certainly did not act intentionally, in permitting their dog to run at large?" I asked Harry; my only knowledge of criminal defense was from law school.

"They owned the dog and since they haven't offered a plea, I really think the district attorney is looking for someone to hang the blame on. They have a dead body and a town in an uproar. They're going to need closure on this one," Harry explained.

"How much will it cost for you to defend them?" I asked.

"At least ten thousand dollars," he answered.

The tears continued to roll. "We don't have that kind of money," Teri cried. Her husband and children were in tears around her. Harry said he was sorry and left my office while I finished my conference with the family. I knew I could defend these people for less than ten thousand dollars. And I believed I could get them off. They hadn't known their dog was vicious, they hadn't secured him in a negligent manner, and I felt I could create a reasonable doubt as to the cause of the death of the child. I felt sorry for them. All they had done was own a dog, and because of the actions of the dog they were in this terrible situation. I had to do something.

"I'll take your case," I told a surprised and relieved family, "and it won't cost you ten thousand dollars."

I knew I would need help on this one. I set up a meeting with Detective Mike Somer of the county sheriff's department so I could review the evidence. I went to the sheriff's department where Somer led us into a closed room with two-way glass. The detective brought the sealed bags carrying the evidence which they had against Dick and his dog Telly.

The evidence seemed to paint a clear picture of what had happened. They had the broken harness that had allowed the dog to escape; there were tufts of dog hair that had been gathered from a fence the dog would have had to climb through to get to where Tim's body was found. There were the photographs of the boy's body with apparent bite marks. But, searching through the papers and photographs, I felt there was other evidence such as other bruises on the child that left important questions unanswered.

How had the boy gotten out of the house unnoticed? Why had the front door of the house been deadbolt-locked in the morning? Why had the boy not been discovered for nearly seven hours? Why would a ten-year-old, with no pants on and no shoes, run down a dirt road in the middle of a cold October night? Why did the autopsy indicate a bruise to the head and a gash across the forehead, both of which were indicated as being non-dog-related injuries?

There were other possible scenarios. Had someone abused the child? The father had a history of spousal abuse. Had the father locked the child out of the house? He had done that on prior occasions to punish the boy. Was the father even home at the time the child chased down the street after his mother, or had he come home afterwards and locked the door behind him? Had the dog come upon the body of the boy after he had been killed by a car? Had wild animals such as coyotes attacked the boy, and the dog showed up after his death? Had other dogs been at the scene? These were all questions whirling through my mind, questions I would need to investigate in order to prepare a defense for my client. One way or another, I was going to be sure that my client did not go to jail over a crime that was based on circumstantial evidence and, even then, committed by his dog.

One day while the case was still pending, I got on the elevator in my building and ran into Jerry Burden. I had met Jerry through a friend I had gone to law school with, but had never really had the chance to get to know him.

"Are you in this building?" he asked me as the elevator rose.

"Yes," I responded. "I just moved my offices up to the seventeenth floor. Would you like to come up for a tour?"

"Well." He hesitated. "I'm really busy, but I guess so."

He reluctantly followed me up to my office, was introduced around, and quickly disappeared. So I was surprized the next day when I received a bouquet of roses along with an invitation for dinner. At dinner I told him about the case in Corella. He was fascinated that dog law involved so much investigating. He asked if he could offer his services, and I accepted.

We began dating and several weekends later Jerry and I traveled to Corella, Colorado, thirty miles south of Denver. Walking around, we discovered the only restaurants in town were a truck stop and a burger joint. There was one bar and two roadside motels. We picked one of the motels and checked in for the night. Jerry had more experience investigating cases like this than I did and he suggested we talk to the people in town and learn what they knew. That night we went to the bar and talked to the locals.

"What did you think about that little boy dying up here last fall?" I asked a man seated at the bar.

"That was a tragedy. Everyone was real sad about that."

"I knew that boy," another man chimed in. "My son went to school with him."

"Do you know what caused his death?" Jerry asked, getting right to the point as I cringed waiting for an answer.

"They say a dog killed him."

"But what was he doing out in the middle of the night?" Jerry probed.

"They say he was chasing after his mother."

"This is getting us nowhere," I whispered to Jerry. "These guys are just repeating what they read in the newspapers."

We continued to discuss the case but didn't learn anything we didn't already know. We didn't want to attract too much suspicion to ourselves so we left early and went back to the motel. Standing out in front of the motel with Jerry and looking over the plains of the dark farm community, the solitude and quietness of the area hit me.

"This place is very lonely and desolate for a ten-year-old boy to be out alone in the middle of the night."

Jerry nodded. "Come on. We can't solve this case tonight. Let's go to bed."

With his arm around me we walked into our tiny room and forgot the case for the rest of the night.

The next morning I began wondering again what had really happened to Tim Taylor. We had breakfast at the diner. In speaking to the waitress we learned some interesting facts about the boy's mother. According to this source, the mother had been having an affair with a local deputy police officer. The father had also had a girlfriend. The more I learned, the more questions I had about the family. It was looking more likely that no one was home the night the boy ran from the house.

Jerry and I then drove across town to the home of Nancy Farragan, an emergency technician. She had been one of the first people to see little Tim's body. We hoped she could shed some light on the circumstances surrounding the boy's death.

"It was the worst thing I had ever seen," she told us as her three kids and two dogs ran around at our feet.

"How long have you been an emergency technician?" I asked her.

"That was my first day," she told me. Which didn't help in qualifying her as an expert in determining what had happened.

"What did you see when you got to the scene?" I asked, hoping to find more leads.

"The boy's body was lying by the side of the road. Besides the scratch marks, the boy wasn't in bad shape. But what surprised me the most was the father's reaction. He didn't seem upset at all. He just stared at the boy." It was obvious that Ms. Farragan had no great love for Ralph Taylor.

"Do you think the bites to the boy caused his death?" Jerry questioned her, always getting to the point faster than I was ready for the answer.

"I don't know," she responded. "But it looked like he could have been hit by a car or even beaten and dumped there. You know, his father was having an affair." She told us this like she was letting us in on a great secret. But the parents' affairs had not been too secret.

I went to the county sheriff's department and pulled the criminal record on Ralph Taylor. He had been charged with domestic violence for a fight with his wife. He was set to appear in court the following week. I decided to show up to watch the proceedings. I needed to know more about the father of the young victim.

The following week I went to court only to learn that Ralph Taylor wasn't going to appear. He had skipped town. The last anyone had heard from him, he was headed for a tropical island. A bench warrant was put out for his arrest. Tim's mother and baby sister had also moved out of state. My clients were left to deal with their defense, and the scrutiny of the town, on their own. The case was set for a preliminary hearing to determine what would be the issues at the trial.

The prosecutor, the judge and I all met in the judge's chambers. The state's burden was to prove that my client had "knowingly or negligently permitted his dog to run at large causing injury or death to a person." I felt that our best chance at a defense was to establish that my client had not acted either "knowingly or negligently." I moved for a ruling that the dog having been at large in and of itself did not establish negligence but, rather, negligence would have to be proven by the prosecution. The judge agreed.

To establish negligence, the prosecution would have to prove that my client acted or failed to act in a manner that he should have known would result in his dog running at large. They therefore had to prove that Dick was negligent in the way he had secured Telly before going to bed. We would have to show that there was no way that Dick could have known that Telly would escape from the manner in which he had been restrained. The prosecution had the harness which had apparently broken, allowing the dog to run free. We had to show that the harness was a reasonable means of securing the dog. I felt we had a stronger case after the judge determined that the prosecution needed to prove Dick's actual negligence. I returned to the courtroom to tell Dick, Teri and their family that so far things were working in their favor. They did not appear relieved. They were depressed over little Tim's death and the lurking questions about them and their pet. They wanted the case over and it just seemed to be dragging on. We set the case for trial for the following month. We had four weeks to exhaust all possible defenses.

During this time, Jerry had been scheduled to meet with Detective Somer one more time. After the meeting he rushed over to my office in a panic.

"We need to talk," he said as he swung my office door closed to prevent the secretarial staff I shared with six other attorneys from overhearing him. After the negative opinion of the case from attorney Harry Hopkin, the rest of the attorneys and staff were surprised that I had taken the case. Jerry and I made every effort to keep the progress, or lack of it, quiet. But with the media covering our every move—the case was the first trial of a dog owner for his dog's alleged murder—the nightly news reports were filled with the case.

"My meeting with Somer didn't go well," Jerry began. "Things don't look good for Dick."

"What are you talking about?" I said. "I don't think Dick was responsible."

Jerry frowned. "Maybe not, but I was looking at the harness that they have as evidence. You know, the blue horse harness?"

"Right," I replied, wanting him to continue.

"And I was reconstructing it to see how it had secured the dog. We had assumed it had fit the dog the same way a dog harness would have, right?"

I nodded.

"Well, it couldn't have been on the dog that way."

"Why not?"

"Because there is a piece missing and it would not have been able to restrain the dog if it had been on over his head."

"So what are you telling me?"

"That the harness could not have been on the dog."

"Oh come on," I said. "We're too close to being able to destroy the prosecution's case for negligence to start conjecturing crazy ideas about the dog's harness."

"I'm serious." Jerry defended his theory. "When I was with Detective Somer he realized the same thing when I was piecing together what the harness would have looked like whole."

My temper flared. "You did tests on the harness in front of the prosecution's witness?" I was getting angry at Jerry now. Not only was he destroying my client's defense, but he was supposed to help me and he was showing his discovery to the prosecution.

"He was just there with me. We had been talking about the harness and how it had restrained the dog, but when we put it back together, it didn't work like a harness."

"Maybe a piece is still missing?" I asked hopefully.

"Somer says they searched everywhere for the pieces and what they have is all there was. Besides, he said the edges of the harness straps are so worn that it would have been a long time ago that those pieces broke away."

"So now they are going to be able to show that the harness could not have restrained the dog?"

"Yes. We need to find out how the dog had really been restrained."

"I'll call the Ryders."

I immediately called Teri Ryder at work and scheduled a visit with the family at their home the next day, a Saturday. I did not tell her what the visit was about.

Jerry and I drove there together. I was still barely speaking to him.

Teri was waiting at the door. "We're all anxious about your visit. What's the matter?" she asked, trembling.

I didn't want to alarm them but there were some questions I had to have answers for.

"We need to go over the way in which Telly was restrained," I said calmly. "Can we see where he was kept?"

"Sure," Dick responded as he led us out to the back-yard. To the side of the yard there was a doghouse. We walked over.

"This is where he stayed at night," Dick explained. "We secured him to the house with a chain. The police took the chain."

We had examined the chain and there was no question that it was still intact and had not been what caused Telly to get free. The harness had been found still latched to the chain when the police had taken the items as evidence.

"How was Telly attached to the chain?" I asked. Although we had been over this before in my office we had never reviewed the facts on location.

"The harness was latched to the chain," Dick answered.

"Who attached Telly to the chain that night?" I asked, trying to put the picture together.

"Sam did. It was his job." Sam was standing next to Dick. I hadn't questioned the children, who were very upset, in the two months I had been representing their father, although we had seen each other many times.

Sam was a chubby eleven-year-old with blond hair, and very shy.

"Tell me how you attached him." I directed my question to Sam. Hesitantly, he began to describe how the harness had been attached to the chain.

"The harness went over his head and then I latched the chain to the piece under his chin."

Dick interrupted. "That's not how you did it. I'll show

you how it was done." Dick showed how the dog had been harnessed by the chain by attaching it to the metal loop on the top of the harness, the loop that would be on the side of a horse's head. That would have been the most secure way of restraining the dog, but, based upon Jerry's investigation, we now knew that the piece of harness from one metal loop to the other and the other metal loop was missing. The harness could not have been secured in that manner. The boy looked at the ground while Dick continued to speak for him. It was apparent that he didn't want his father to know what really happened. When I explained to the father that the harness could not have worked in the way he described, he got very defensive.

"Maybe they haven't found all the pieces."

But we had already exhausted that possibility. I explained to him that the prosecutor would see right through any explanation that didn't match the evidence. I asked Sam to show me again how he thought the dog had been harnessed. This time he repeated exactly what his father had just told us. The entire time he was speaking Dick kept staring at him. I didn't know why Dick felt he had to hide the truth from me, but I knew he was lying to me.

"I can't take the issue to trial without the truth," I said.

But they only became more silent.

I could see by the fear in their faces how scared they were. They knew their dog had been at large that night and they knew a boy had been killed. It was obvious Dick was protecting his son and wasn't going to be dissuaded. I had to work with what I had.

Back at my office, I called the prosecuting attorney and discussed the negligence issue. I told him about the domestic violence at the dead boy's house and the fact that

Ralph Taylor had skipped the country. I then asked him to give us a lesser plea before I took the case to trial. I was bluffing. There was no way I could let the family take the case to trial when it was really Sam who'd failed to secure the dog. Though he was a minor there was enough doubt as to negligence without letting my client get on the stand where he'd have to demonstrate his story of how the harness had been attached, when I knew his story didn't hold water. I had to protect him before trial.

I was sure the district attorney knew of the faulty harness. But I could tell as I continued speaking he felt sorry for Dick Ryder. Dick had had no reason to believe his dog would attack a child. And if there had been any negligence in securing Telly to his chain, it had been Dick's son, Sam, who had acted negligently. Despite all this, I breathed a sigh of relief when the prosecutor offered a plea to a lesser charge that would involve no jail time and a minimal fine.

"That sounds fair," I said, "but let me talk to my client."

Dick Ryder accepted the plea. The case was over and soon afterwards the family moved out of state.

The case had been my first dog law trial in Colorado and it had been heart-wrenching. I would never forget the troubled family that had lost a son nor the father I had defended who was willing to sacrifice himself to save his own child.

The only bright spot was that a case involving an animal had received respect and consideration from the court, the prosecutor, the detectives, and the media. It had not been treated as a "dog" case but as a serious legal matter. Now I had hope that the Colorado courts would look more open-mindedly at other animal rights cases as well.

By the end of the case Jerry and I had become quite close. Once we had started dating we never stopped. Now we needed a break together away from the case.

"I have some business next weekend in Telluride," Jerry told me. "Would you like to drive out there with me?"

I agreed and Dar, Anke, Jerry and I drove the seven hours across the mountains to Telluride. Finally, the dogs and I had a male companion to travel with. After an enjoyable weekend in Telluride, I called my secretary first thing Monday morning to tell her I would not be back until Tuesday.

"But you have to come back," Lisa told me in a panic-stricken voice. "I've booked you on the Joan Rivers Show."

"When?" I asked, alarmed.

"Tomorrow," she responded.

"How am I supposed to be in New York by tomorrow?" I asked while I was trying to figure out the answer myself. Not only did I have a seven-hour drive in front of me, I had two dogs with me, and a four-hour flight to New York.

"You'll figure it out," Lisa assured me. "I have you booked on the last flight out tonight, returning tomorrow after the show. They want to talk to you about dogs and divorce."

I had recently been interviewed by the New York Times for an article about dog custody disputes, and Joan Rivers had apparently seen the article and wanted to learn more. We began the drive across the mountains by 10:00 a.m. After seven exhausting hours of traveling and two confused dogs, we dropped the dogs in the backyard with their dog door to the house opened and quickly packed one suit and one traveling outfit for New York. We had been told that a limousine would meet us at La Guardia Airport. Jerry, having never been to New York City, thought his western ways would be well received.

When no limousine was apparent at the airport, he told me, "Wait right here" as he wandered up the line of cabs. I watched him go, wondering what he had in mind. Within minutes I saw his hands flying up in the air and I rushed to grab him away from the irate Haitian cab driver who had not taken too kindly to Jerry's insult about non-English-speaking cab drivers who didn't know where the limousines to the Joan River's Show were. I made a point to keep a closer eye on Jerry for the rest of the trip. I dragged him back to the private car area and soon our driver arrived to take us to the Plaza Hotel.

The following morning we were driven to the show in another limousine. The title of the show was "Unusual Professions." I was not aware of who the other guests were. Once the limousine pulled up, I quickly realized that the transvestite in the leopard fur coat, the man dressed in the chicken suit, and a gay couple were going to be accompanying us to the show. I quickly jumped in the front seat with the driver and left Jerry to fend for himself in the back with the other guests.

It was a successful show. Joan Rivers took dog law very seriously, and I received applause from the audience for my work in representing dog owners' rights, not the laughs and jeers I had feared. We returned on our own to the Plaza. We looked at each other and I said, "So what do you want to do now?"

"Well, we are in New York," Jerry ventured.

"And the leaves are changing," I continued.

"No use going back now," Jerry finished for me.

Linda Cawley

We had never seen Autumn changing in New England. It would be a great trip to spend some non-business time together. There were only two problems: 1) We had no other clothes, and 2) The dogs were in the backyard in Colorado. I quickly called my kennel and asked them to retrieve the dogs for me. They were the only ones brave enough to go into a secured yard where there were two German shepherds and take them out of the yard by going over the fence, but they succeeded. Then we rented a car in midtown Manhattan and drove north into Connecticut. We quickly found a Gap clothing store and purchased outfits for the rest of the trip. Now we were ready to enjoy New England in the autumn. It was my first road trip without dogs.

We ate lobster in Mystic, Connecticut, toured mansions in Providence, Rhode Island, got lost in Boston, got spooked in Salem, saw incredible foliage in New Hampshire and had the time of our lives. We forgot about all the work we had left behind and enjoyed each other's company.

After the New England trip we knew we were in love. On New Year's Eve Jerry proposed and I accepted. We planned to get married the following fall. But there were more cases to be completed in the meantime.

7

"Really, Your Honor, He Didn't Mean to Bite Her"

The defense of a dog is like no other criminal defense. Whether the dog has already been incarcerated, is on home probation, or is on death row, the charged dog needs legal assistance and so does his owner. Although it is the owner who is charged with the "crime," it is the dog who committed the bad act and the dog who is sent to "jail" or executed.

Most vicious dog charges require that there be a "bite or attack" by a dog against a person or another domestic animal, and the bite or attack be unprovoked. Because of the requirement that the bite be unprovoked, provocation is the usual grounds for defense. But even if there was provocation, the dog's reaction must be reasonable. Too often owners rely on provocation out of fear that it is the only defense available to them.

One wintry day I met with Carol Conway who lived in a suburb which had become notorious for its dog laws disfavoring the dog owner. Carol and her husband, Larry, had a

Siberian husky which had been taken away by animal control. Carol had been walking her dog, Harry, along the sidewalks within their apartment complex. Harry was on a four-foot leash. When Nancy Todd, a neighbor, passed the dog, the dog lunged forward and bit the woman. It was Harry's second bite, and the city attorney wanted the dog to be put to death. In searching for a defense, I asked Carol whether there was any way we could argue that the woman did something to provoke the dog.

"Oh yes," she responded, encouraged by the possibility of a defense. "Harry knew this woman. She and her children live above us, and the children shoot rubber bands down on Harry. We've found the rubber bands on our patio. So when Mrs. Todd walked by, I'm sure Harry knew that this was the mother of those nasty children, and he bit her."

It was a novel point but I knew this argument for provocation would never fly in front of a jury. We took a plea for a lesser charge. Harry never got to go home again, but the charges against Carol were dropped. Sometimes the living arrangement is not right for the dog and the dog will only be in more trouble if it returns home. In this case, the dog couldn't live cooped up on a patio in an apartment complex. It was just setting the dog up for trouble, as well as the owner.

Sometimes, owners can go to great lengths to create an argument for provocation. A few weeks later I had an appointment for a client consultation with a Mrs. Wardlow, an attractive blond-haired woman in her early forties. Dressed in a chic gray suit as though she were attending a social function, she sat down in my office. Immediately she began to cry. "My beloved Akita has been taken away for allegedly biting a six-year-old child."

"Tell me how it happened," I said gently and handed her the Kleenex box I keep nearby.

"I have six sons," she went on. "The oldest is twelve and the youngest is two. My six-year-old had a playmate over and the two boys went into the backyard. My son left his friend alone in the backyard with Superboy, and the next thing we heard was screaming. My husband and I ran outside and saw the boy lying spreadeagled, face down in the dirt. Superboy was on top of him. He had bitten the boy from the front of the head back over the scalp. My husband, John, pulled the dog off."

I shivered. The story gave me chills just thinking about a one-hundred-fifty-pound dog on top of a small child. I had just become engaged to and, Jerry, and made a mental note to be sure we never owned an Akita after we had children.

"This sounds serious," I told Mrs. Wardlow. "What would you like me to do?"

"I want my dog back," she answered to my surprise. "They want to destroy him and I don't think he should be put to sleep."

"But you have six children at home. Why would you want this dog back?" I asked.

"Oh, he's not really vicious," she defended him. "He knew this boy was a troublemaker. A few months ago this boy started a fire in the neighborhood. Other mothers won't let their children play with him. When Superboy saw the boy alone in the yard, he probably thought he was a threat to my family."

"So the dog scalped him?" I asked, pointing out that her conclusion was illogical in light of the circumstances. She had no answer. I shook my head. "I'm sorry, I don't think there's anything a six-year-old could do in the eyes of the court that would provoke a dog to scalp him. With so many children in the house, all of whom undoubtedly have 'troublesome' friends, I can't in good conscience try to get the dog returned home.

"I just can't take your case," I told Mrs. Wardlow, concluding the consultation. "I don't think this animal should be in your home."

She began to cry again, this time even harder. "But I bought the dog for my husband when he quit hitting us. We celebrate his being born again every year on Superboy's birthday. It's been two years now."

So that explained her real concern. She was afraid that if the dog wasn't there as a constant reminder to her husband that he not hit anyone, he might start battering again. I felt sorry for the woman but I think she was relieved to know that a vicious dog would not be returning to her home. I couldn't guarantee that a vicious husband wouldn't.

Another case which I almost refused to defend occurred when Jenny Sorita, a thirtyish, plump but pretty woman, walked into my office one Thursday morning. "The animal control wants to put my dog to sleep because Sir allegedly bit my niece."

"What kind of a dog is it?" I asked.

"A collie," she answered.

"A collie?" I repeated, perplexed. "That surprises me," I said. "Having been raised with a collie, I'm a lover of the breed. I've never encountered a collie that was vicious towards children. I'll take the case and investigate later."

My fiancé Jerry continued helping me on cases. He hadn't taken dog law seriously when we first got together, but after a few months he was as captivated as I was and offered his continued help. There was a lot of work to be done which required the assistance of an investigator. That afternoon, Jerry and I went to the animal control kennels where Jenny Sorita's dog was being incarcerated. The veterinarian there, Dr. Wells, was an acquaintance of mine. I had worked with him on other legal cases and he was familiar with my work. He knew that if I was visiting a dog on "death row," I was considering defending the dog's owner.

"Do you have a collie here on a vicious dog charge?" I asked him.

"A collie?" he answered. "What's the name?"

"Sir," I told him, and he raised his eyebrows.

"I don't think you want to visit that dog. He's in our vicious dog section. He's a real dangerous one," Dr. Wells warned us.

"Oh great," Jerry said, "just what you need."

"I've already taken the case," I whispered. Then I turned to Dr. Wells. "I have to see the dog."

Dr. Wells frowned but escorted us back to the cage where dogs on death row were kept. "Stay behind the fence barricading the vicious dogs from the other animals," he said, pointing to Jerry. I peered inside the six-foot caged run. There was a dog about twenty inches high with a short tan and white coat and a white spot around one reddened eye. His tail curled up over his back, and he stood with the stocky stance of a pit bull with teeth bared.

"Sir." He ignored me. "Come here, Sir."

The dog frothed, staring off into vacant space, still ignoring me. Nothing would have caused me to put my hand into that cage. A non-reacting dog can be more dangerous than a snapping and growling one.

Now I didn't know what to do. I had promised Jenny Sorita I would defend Sir. But I had to think of both my reputation and standards. I was known for having a perfect success record in the courts. Burt Benton, the city attorney who handled the majority of dog law cases, and I had on many occasions negotiated cases. Benton had once been described to me as "Colorado's dog prosecutor."

We liked and often teased each other about our identities as Dog Defense Attorney and Dog Prosecutor. He had often dismissed my clients because he knew I did not take cases when the dog was really vicious. He relied upon me to go to animal control, check the dogs, and only argue on behalf of those who were safe. Now I had to defend a case in which I didn't believe the dog was innocent. I didn't think I could do that. I decided to tell Mrs. Sorita I could not take her and Sir's case. She was scheduled to return to my office the following morning.

By the time she got there, I had prepared what I would tell her as to why I could not take her case. Before I could speak, she handed me an armload of videotapes.

"Here," she said. "These are tapes of Sir so you can get to know him better."

She didn't know I had already seen him. I put the tapes into the VCR. On the television screen came an animated version of Sir I had not seen. He was playful and gentle as he romped around the yard with the client's two small children and her niece. The children couldn't have been happier, nor could the dog. The dog on that videotape was an entirely different animal than the one I had seen in animal control. It was apparent to me that the family loved the dog and the dog loved his family. I realized then that a dog incarcerated is entirely different from a dog with his family. In seeing the dog from his family's point of view, I realized that Sir was someone's beloved pet, not just a caged vicious animal. The family loved Sir and he didn't appear to be a danger to them. I took the case, and we got a dismissal. The dog returned home.

At the same time as Mrs. Sorita's and Sir's case, I was fighting another case in which the owners, Betty and Bob Steiner, insisted that their dog, Billie, had been provoked into biting a seven-year-old girl. The dog, a medium sized terrier mix, had been tied to their front porch when Nancy Lowell, the daughter of a neighbor, came over. She had been playing nicely with the dog out in the front yard, alone, while her parents visited with the Steiners. "Then she came inside for a little while and said, 'He's a nice doggie.' A few minutes later she headed back out again and we heard commotion. Billie had bitten her."

According to Bob Steiner, Nancy must have jumped off the front porch and landed on Billie's back, thereby startling the dog and causing him to turn and nip Nancy on the arm. According to Nancy, she was just sitting next to Billie petting him when for no reason he turned and bit her. No one witnessed the alleged bite.

"The seven-year-old would have to testify and it's not likely," I said, "that Billie will win over the jury against seven-year-old Nancy. Unless we can get her to reveal the truth, we don't have much of a chance."

Animal control was already moving to have the dog destroyed. Later that day, I talked to animal control officer Kate Rollins, who had a strong argument. "You know," Officer Rollins informed me, "that dog has been vicious before."

I was surprised to hear that the dog had been vicious before because I had searched the city records and there was no record of a prior bite. A second bite would be much more difficult to defend.

"What do you mean?" I questioned her.

"Well, we have had other complaints," Rollins told me. "The neighborhood middle school is only a block away from the Steiners' house. The school principal called us because the kids complained that the dog barks at them when they walk by the house."

"But they have a six-foot privacy fence in their back-yard," I responded. "How can he get over that and be vicious?"

"Well," she answered, "we feel that the dog's barking along the fence could scare the kids on the sidewalk and they might jump out into the street and get hit by a car."

I was shocked. Rollins was going to argue that Billie should be destroyed because kids in the fifth to eighth grade, on the sidewalk outside of a privacy fence, might become so afraid of a barking dog that they would step into the street where a car might just happen to hit them. But if Officer Rollins was going to testify, based on that hypothetical instance, that Billie was vicious we would have to find evidence to counter that opinion.

I told the Steiners what I had been told by Officer Rollins. They were aware of Billie barking at the kids, but said that the kids had been provoking the dog into barking at them. I told them to get me evidence.

At the next hearing, I elaborately opened a large card-board box taking out one by one sticks, rocks, balls, toys, and other things that the children had thrown over the fence to aggravate the dog. But most incriminating were paper air-planes, which had been made from the kids' school papers, *with their names still on them.* The dog was permitted to live, so long as he was kept inside when the kids went to and from school, and kept away from other children. The children were reprimanded when I brought the box to school and showed it to the principal.

At the same time that I was defending these allegedly vicious dogs, I had my own dog problem going on at home. A letter arrived from the United States Postal Service stating that they would not deliver mail to our house, and possibly not to the entire street, because of Dar's "vicious" barking at the mailman. Dar by this time was nearly five years old and I had never had a problem with him barking at mailmen before. So I decided to do my own investigation. When the mail truck pulled up across the street, I went out to the yard to observe. Dar didn't attack the postman, but my one-hun-dred-twenty-pound brave dog slinked off into the garage through his dog door. I had never seen Dar act afraid of any-thing before.

A few days later, I put Dar out in the yard about mail delivery time. I hid in the living room where I could see the mail carrier coming up the street. The backyard has a fence around it, preventing the dogs from going past the front edge of the house. They were standing there watching the mail carrier deliver to the next door neighbor's house. After that house, as the carrier approached our house, instead of walk-ing back out the front walk of the neighbor's house, the post-man began to cut across the yard towards the dogs in the side yard. Dar began barking aggressively and jumping at the fence. The carrier walked right up to him, off the path to our house, and sprayed him in the face with pepper spray. Without even flinching, the carrier then walked back out front where he delivered mail to our house, only to find me at the front door staring at him.

"How could you spray my dog when he was nowhere near you?"

He appeared flustered, "I was told he's vicious."

"How can he be vicious when he's behind a fence?" I felt righteous indignation and took him to task. "You don't have to cut through the yard. You never have to go in the back yard. The only reason he hates mailmen now is because you are spraying him in the face with pepper spray."

The mail carrier looked embarrassed. "I'm not your usual carrier. Ben, your usual carrier, is the one who told me to spray him."

I was ready for a fight now. Here was a mailman admitting that he only sprayed my dog in the face because another carrier had told him to do it. No wonder Dar now hated mailmen. I spoke with the main office and told the supervisor to keep the carriers out of my backyard and especially to keep Ben away from my dogs. Soon after, Ben went on disability leave. No other carrier ever had a problem with the dogs. But I now knew what it was like to have someone wrongfully accuse your dog of being vicious. I wanted to help people in similar situations, and I found such an opportunity only days later.

When Kelly McPherson called my office she explained, "I've already been through two attorneys, thousands of dollars in legal fees, and my dog has been in a kennel for nearly three months at my expense, because of an alleged dog bite." I scheduled her for a consultation. She and her husband Ian arrived at my office holding hands. They were an attractive young couple and seemed to be well organized.

"We're frustrated with the legal system that has held our dog for so long," he explained.

I asked Kelly, who was pert and red-haired, to explain what had happened.

"Ian and our two dogs, McDuffy and McTeague, were out on our property while I was in the house," she began. "I saw a man cross the bridge onto our property. He was walking very determinedly. I didn't recognize him. I went out on the balcony and shouted to him, 'Don't come on the property or the dogs will bite you.'"

"Did he respond?" I questioned.

"No," she said. "He just kept coming. I yelled to him again, 'Get off the property. The dogs are out and they will bite,' but he shrugged his shoulders and kept coming."

"Did you really think the dogs would bite him?" I questioned, thinking the prosecution would construe her statement to mean that she knew her dog was vicious.

"No. But I wasn't sure they wouldn't. We had just moved to this house. It's secluded and up in the mountains and I was afraid of strangers. I hoped by telling him that the dogs would bite he would leave. But I could see Duffy, our male Irish setter, trotting intently toward this stranger in our yard."

"What did Duffy do when he reached the man?"

"At the point he reached the driveway, he was just barking at the stranger. The man raised his arm up in the air. Duffy jumped up at him, barking and snapping. He raised his arm again and Duffy nipped him above the elbow."

"Did the nip tear his sleeve?" I asked.

"He had short sleeves on," she answered. "But the

man wasn't bleeding or anything, and Ian then grabbed Duffy."

"What did the man do when your husband arrived?"

"He asked that we put the dogs inside so he could talk to us."

"Was he upset?" I questioned.

"He was, but he had been upset when he came on the property," she answered. "He yelled about grass clippings and a salt lick we had put on the borders of our property."

"A salt lick?" I was confused.

"We had just moved up to Sagegreen," she responded. Sagegreen is a town twenty miles from Denver in the Rocky Mountains. "We wanted the elk to come near the house so we could see them. His property is just a vacant lot so we didn't think it would hurt anything."

"But that had upset him?" I asked, for clarification.

"Apparently," she responded. "He told us that he didn't want elk on the property and if our dogs ever went on his property he would shoot them."

It appeared that this man did not like animals and didn't care for neighbors too much, either. He was going on their property to give them a piece of his mind. I was thinking that we would have to prove that the dog sensed this and construed the man's raising his arm as provocation.

After Duffy bit him on the arm, a "bite" which hadn't broken the skin and had not drawn blood, the man left the McPherson property. He apparently went home and called the county animal control only to be told that the county laws would not assist him in charging the McPhersons with a crime. In that county, there is no law to prosecute the owner of a dog which bites a trespasser. He continued to look for an avenue to have the McPhersons prosecuted and called the county sheriff's department, requesting information on the dog laws for the State of Colorado. When he learned of the Colorado Vicious Dog Law, a state law available to but not often used by the county, which charged a person with ownership of a dangerous dog even if the alleged victim was bitten while trespassing, he requested that the McPhersons be charged with that crime.

Relying upon the victim's representations that he had been bitten, the sheriff's department sent two officers out to pick up Duffy. Duffy was impounded and quarantined. Kelly was charged with ownership of a dangerous dog. The law, which was less than two years old, had been enacted as a means of controlling vicious dogs without being breed specific. It specifically stated that local communities could enact their own laws, but the state law would always be available to them. The unfortunate aspect of the state law for my clients was that a second count under that law constituted a felony. I felt the dog had provocation and I didn't want Kelly to be found guilty of even one count under the state law.

But my first concern was to get the dog out of the kennel. A catch-22 develops in some jurisdictions where the animal can be incarcerated pending trial of a vicious dog case. By the time the case gets to trial, the dog has been in a kennel for so long that the animal control officer then testifies, "Well, maybe he wasn't vicious when we took him, but he's been in a kennel for three months, and now we know he is vicious."

There was only one chance to get the dog out pending trial, and that was by arguing that the dog himself was evidence in the case and by keeping the dog in the kennel for such a long period of time, the dog himself was being "altered" (in temperament) and therefore the prosecution was in essence destroying evidence. I felt the motion was based on an excellent argument even though I had tried it in cases before with no success. I felt the situation was the same as if the state had confiscated the smoking gun, stored it in a closet where it was deteriorating pending trial, and then going to use it as evidence that the gun used in the crime was in bad shape. Judge Tarshish luckily saw it my way. She permited the dog to go home, and, set a trial date as soon as possible. We were now ready to prep the case for a trial.

I needed to have Duffy evaluated by an animal behaviorist in order to have an expert witness available to testify in support of my theory that the dog had only attacked because he felt he and his family were threatened by the trespasser's attitude and behavior. In a reconstruction of the incident, I wanted to know whether Duffy would have bitten if an aggressive move had not first been made by the trespasser. I scheduled Dr. Margaret Russell, a noted animal behaviorist, for a meeting with the family and the dog. Her husband, Todd Whiting, also an animal behaviorist, was set to participate in the test. We arranged to have the McPhersons at home with Duffy tied at the front door when the animal behaviorists arrived at the property. They would run a series of temperament tests on Duffy.

I wanted to be sure to observe the tests. Jerry, who was now both my husband and investigator, was now working on dog law cases for me on a regular basis. We agreed to meet the McPhersons at their home to observe the tests and then go out to dinner. Jerry and I rushed up to Sagegreen after work. We parked out of sight from the front door. Through the glass panel when I rang the doorbell, I saw an Irish setter who was barking loudly. He was the size of a cheetah and charged the front door. "Oh no," I murmured. "There is no way this dog won't be considered vicious."

Duffy was a long-haired, large-boned Irish setter and he was showing all of his strength that night. Ian pulled him away from the door and he settled down enough for us to enter the home. Although Jerry had been perfecting his ability to get the alleged vicious dog to be friendly with him, I didn't see the point. There would be no way I could defend a dog in court if I was swathed in bandages from being attacked. Much less if the prosecution ever got hold of medical records showing that it was the dog I was defending who had bitten me. I stayed away from Duffy. He lay at our feet while we discussed the case. At 6:30 p.m., on schedule, Ian leashed Duffy to the front door. A few minutes later we saw the headlights of Drs. Whiting and Russell coming in the McPhersons' driveway. They parked the car right in front of Duffy. Kelly and I went upstairs to the balcony where Kelly had been standing the day of the bite. The others watched from downstairs. No one knew what Whiting and Russell were planning to do, or what Duffy's reaction would be.

As Todd Whiting exited the car Duffy barked aggressively. The doctor acted suspiciously as he approached the dog by covering his face and stopping and starting. The dog continued to bark. Suddenly Todd jumped forward and stomped on the ground. Duffy backed up, continuing to bark. Then Margaret exited the car and began talking to Todd, ignoring the dog. He began to settle down, barking, but not as aggressively. Soon he was backing towards the house and ignoring the strangers in the front yard who were ignoring him. After the dog calmed down, Todd again approached Duffy in a threatening manner. Duffy barked but kept backing up. "Ian," Dr. Whiting called, "bring Duffy inside." Whiting and Russell followed.

The animal behaviorists explained their observations, Whiting first. "Duffy is a 'fear' biter. He'll only bite when threatened or backed into a corner. He's not outwardly aggressive enough to instigate an attack on his own."

"I agree," said Russell.

Their conclusions supported my arguments and they agreed to testify as expert witnesses at the trial. Although they had determined that Duffy was very protective, they would testify that he would not attack unless he felt threatened or thought his owners were threatened. I now had one argument of defense.

Another avenue for defense was the requirement of the law that a bite be such as "to require medical treatment." I pulled the state's file to determine what evidence they had of medical treatment. According to the records, the victim, who was named Walt Jackson, had sought medical treatment at an emergency care clinic in Sagegreen three days after the incident.

Driving over to the clinic, I pulled the medical records. They indicated that Jackson had been seen and treated for a dog bite. What was unusual was that no treatment had been indicated. No therapy, no stitches, no prescriptions, no medical doctor had ever seen the patient. Going further, I obtained the name of the nurse who had treated Jackson.

I called Nurse Stedman on the telephone and informed her that I was the attorney for the owners of a dog that had allegedly bitten Walt Jackson. "Do you recall treating him for a dog bite on May 10, 1993?" I asked her.

"Yes," she responded. "Actually I do." I was surprised that she would remember the victim whom she had seen nearly three months earlier.

"Did you treat his injury?" I proceeded.

"Well, I remember the incident because he really didn't have any injury. He came into the emergency care clinic and told me he had been bitten by a dog. He showed me his arm where he claimed he had been bitten, but there was no bite mark. There was nothing at all."

"What treatment did you recommend for him?" I continued.

"None actually," she answered. "I told him to go home and rest it but that there was nothing I could do for him."

"Do you remember or could you have had a doctor see the patient?" I asked carefully, since the answer would be so critical to our defense.

"No," she said as I breathed a sigh of relief. "I didn't think he needed a doctor."

"Therefore," I continued slowly, wanting to get her conclusion, "would it be correct to say the patient never received any medical treatment from you or any doctor that you know of?"

"That's correct," she answered. Thanking her, I hung up and gave a sigh of relief. Without medical treatment, the injury did not qualify as a "bite" under state law.

I prepared my case for trial, trying to cover every angle. I had named eight witnesses. There were Kelly and Ian, Duffy's owners. I had Dr. Margaret Russell, the expert witness animal behaviorist. I had the nurse who would testify that there had been no medical treatment. I had State Veterinarian Colby Hanson on hand to testify that he had examined the dog and had seen many vicious dogs and this dog was not vicious as the law had intended. I had an animal control expert, Richard Rosen, scheduled to testify as to the intent of the law, since he had had a hand in the drafting of the law. I had the kennel owner and her son who had cared for Duffy for the past three months available to testify as to his nature.

What I had going against me was a prosecuting district attorney and a judge who, I believed, each wanted to execute my client. The prosecutor was Tony Esposito whom I had met in another barking dog case, one where it had been apparent halfway through the trial that the dispute was really over other issues between the neighbors. The judge had pressured the district attorney to offer my clients a plea, any plea. Now Tony wanted revenge.

The judge in the case, Carol Tarshish, was the same judge I had been scheduled to appear before only weeks earlier. My client in that case had been a defendant charged with the wrongful taking of a dog. She had repossessed a puppy she had bred and sold because it had been mistreated and neglected. I had promised to keep the cost low and get her the right to keep the dog. However, I was unable to do so because, when we and our six witnesses appeared for trial, the judge had gone to lunch. Because of the uproar I had caused in the clerk's office after learning that there was no judge to hear the case, Judge Tarshish had been under the mistaken impression that I was going to file a grievance against her. I never did, but because she believed that I had, I felt I might be in for a rough time in her courtroom.

Tony Esposito began his case by having the victim testify.

"How were you injured?" he asked.

"I was bitten on the upper arm."

"Can you show us where?"

"Here." Jackson pointed to his arm. I couldn't see any visible mark.

"Did you receive medical treatment for your injury?" Esposito asked, trying to nail the elements of the crime.

"Yes," Jackson answered. "I was treated by the emergency care clinic in Sagegreen."

On cross-examination, I left the medical treatment alone. I needed to keep his answer as it was for my witness, Nurse Stedman.

Esposito then called the animal control officer who picked up Duffy for incarceration.

"How was his behavior?" he asked.

"He was very vicious," the officer responded. "I thought he was going to come through the glass." She was referring to the glass panel next to the McPhersons' front door. I had heard Duffy barking at that same location when I approached the house, and I knew what she meant. But that wasn't relevant to whether Jackson had been bitten.

I first called Kelly and Ian McPherson to testify as to what had happened. Then I called Richard Rosen to explain what the intent of the law was in regards to defending a dog bite.

"In order to avoid frivolous claims," Rosen testified, "the law defined bite to mean any injury that required medical treatment."

"And what was intended by 'medical treatment?'" I questioned.

"Treatment requiring a doctor, such as stitches."

I then called Nurse Stedman. She testified to what she

had told me previously: "No medical treatment was needed because there was no visible injury."

After Nurse Stedman testified, Judge Tarshish interrupted the proceedings.

"Ms. Cawley," she addressed me, "I have heard enough. It is up to your client but we do not need to go any further. I am prepared to rule."

"Can we take a five-minute recess so I can confer with her?"

"Granted," Tarshish said.

We had not yet called the witnesses as to Duffy's good temperament, or the veterinarians, or the animal behaviorists, but I knew that when a judge interrupts the proceedings so early she usually is on the defense's side. However with this judge, because of my prior history, I could not be completely sure of anything, and I had to let my client make the final decision. Out in the hall I spoke with Kelly briefly. "The odds are very good that we'll win and that to continue with another day and a half of testimony when the judge has already said that she has made up her mind can only sway her unfavorably to change her mind. Because we have so many heavy hitter witnesses yet to come, I'm reluctant to close, but I think it can only help us."

We closed our case.

Within minutes the judge rendered a verdict of not guilty.

The next vicious dog case I was to set for trial was a New York case. Hal and Mary Trent, the clients, were so concerned that their dog, who had bitten people twice previously, would be put to sleep that they were willing to fly Jerry and me to New York to defend them. My female German shepherd, Anke, had died the spring before, and my husband

and I wanted to buy a Shiloh shepherd from a kennel in New York. The puppy would be ready about the same time the case was scheduled for trial. I arranged to fly into Syracuse, drive south to the kennels to get the puppy, and then drive with the puppy to just north of New York City to Peekskill.

When I arrived at the kennels, the breeder had a ring of puppies in the center of the yard. The father of the puppies was chained to a tree, and the mother and older sibling were chained to another tree. As I approached the puppies all of the dogs barked wildly. The breeder showed me the pups. There were two females and one male remaining. I had reserved a female so we would have another companion for Dar. The puppies were all little balls of fur. Shilohs are generally larger than shepherds and have longer coats. We wanted a Shiloh this time around because of their mellow temperaments. Now that I was married, we were planning children soon and wanted a dog that was friendly with children. This dog would be around a long time and we needed a good family pet. I asked the breeder if I could go see the father of the puppies.

"Well," she said hesitantly. "We can try."

I followed her towards the sire who was lunging at the end of his chain.

"Smoky," she shouted at him, "quiet down." There was no way I could even get within an arm's length of the dog without risking losing my arm. I couldn't believe that this vicious dog had sired the puppies. Shilohs are closely regulated in their breedings, but this breeding had been accidental. The intended sire had not been able to get to the dam before Smoky got there, and therefore the puppies only cost $750. Other Shiloh puppies cost as much as $2500. I had decided the less expensive puppies would be fine. Now, looking at the sire, I wasn't sure. But, in observing the dam who was very affectionate as was the sibling, I felt that Smoky's viciousness was more from lack of socialization than genetics.

I observed the puppies playing and interacting. I tested their temperaments for soundness and confidence. I wanted the most outgoing of the puppies, and the sibling female was rather shy. Of all the puppies the one to win me over was a male. Even though my husband and I had agreed to get a female, the male was too great to leave behind. I knew he was the right dog for us, and the breeder agreed to allow me to take him. I packed him into the car and headed for New York with my new puppy, Tucker.

Upon arriving in Peekskill, I checked into the local motel. I had to pick Jerry up at Newark Airport that evening. Tucker and I drove to Newark. We had traveled more than four hundred miles across the state of New York. I had hoped that the travel in the car would be like my first trip with Dar when he was only nine weeks old. We would bond and he would forever love the car as Dar had. Unfortunately, from the start, Tucker hated the car. His long coat would cause him to get too hot, and he would sleep on the floor after pouring his water dish on the carpet of the rental car. I had to keep the air conditioner at full blast all of the time.

The next day, I went to Mr. and Mrs. Trent's home to confer and examine their dog, Ricko. Because of two prior bites, I knew I couldn't get them off completely. But I was going to fight to let them keep the dog. Many people are unaware that in most areas it is legal to own a so-called "vicious dog," so long as the dog is properly confined and warning signs are properly posted, such as with guard dogs. When I arrived at the home, Ricko was tied in the backyard. After talking with the Trents, an older couple in their seventies, we were led to the backyard to meet Ricko. As Mr. Trent led the dog to us holding his collar, Ricko, a male German shepherd mix, lunged at me snapping his jaws. I froze. Looking at his bared teeth, I had no doubt this dog was vicious. I thought he would bite me if I moved. After seeing the dog, I encouraged the Trents to accept a plea of guilty in exchange for the city permitting the dog to remain in their home. At home he would be confined to a run with six-foot side fencing and a roof. Beware of the Dog signs were also required to be posted. The next day in court the plea was accepted.

Vicious dog cases do not always involve an alleged bite to a person. Sometimes the law also includes attacks on other domestic animals to constitute evidence of a dog's viciousness. But, often, dog versus dog scuffles are the nature of the dog, not anything that constitutes viciousness.

Months later I defended a somewhat similar case, but with one big difference: the alleged vicious dogs I defended were actually wolves. The same vicious dog law that was used in Duffy's case was used to charge Gail Franklin, the owner of two wolf hybrids, with ownership of a dangerous dog. The two wolves had escaped from an enclosure on her mountain property. They then proceeded to wander the mountainside, passing by a home with two komondors. Komondors are a large protective sheepherding breed. Being protective of their property, the two komondors charged at the end of their driveway where they encountered the two wolf hybrids. The animals fought until the owner of the komondors called his dogs back onto his property. He then called animal control. According to animal control, when they arrived, one of the komondors, weighing at least one hundred fifty pounds was "limping" from an alleged injured foot. The dog was never taken to a veterinarian and never obtained medical treatment. Once again I argued that without medical treatment, even for an animal, the vicious dog law was inapplicable since it specifically required medical treatment. The prosecutor agreed to drop charges so long as the wolves were confined securely.

In my next dog versus dog attack a woman had been walking her dog along a neighborhood street. The sidewalks were snow covered and icy. At the time she rounded the corner onto my clients' block, Carl and Nina French were arriving home in their van specially equipped for the handicapped with their dog, Silky. Silky, a golden retriever, jumped out of the van off leash. At that same time, the neighbor's two golden retrievers charged past Silky and ran up to the dog being walked. Silky, never leaving his property, joined in the barking and in the chase for the length of his property. No one was bitten but all the commotion caused the dog-walking woman to slip and fall on the ice. She not only filed vicious dog charges against the owner of the other goldens, but against the Frenches. At arraignment, my clients pleaded not guilty. At a hearing before trial, the victim argued that all the dogs had been off leash and charged her causing her dog to make her trip. She was most upset because none of the dog owners came over to help her up. When I explained to her that Silky was a service dog because both my client and his wife were paraplegics and bound to wheelchairs and that Silky had to be off leash to assist them in exiting their van, she wasn't quite so upset. She admitted that only two golden retrievers had approached her, but because she couldn't tell which two of the three had been there, she filed charges against both owners. We moved to have the charges dismissed. The district attorney, Burt Benton, suggested that Silky's owners plead to "aiding and abetting a vicious dog" because Silky had joined in the barking encouraging the encounter by the two neighbor dogs. Because no such charge existed, he agreed to drop the charges.

In vicious dog cases there is great difficulty in deciphering the law. What constitutes an attack? What is provocation to a dog? And what is reasonable under the circumstances? Each jurisdiction treats vicious dog cases differently.

In a landmark case in New Jersey, Taro, an Akita, was incarcerated for more than two years for being an alleged "vicious" dog. Taro was accused of having bitten a young girl, the dog owner's niece. According to Taro's owner, the dog hadn't bitten her but had merely scratched her. Nonetheless, Taro was sentenced to be put to sleep. In New Jersey, dogs are incarcerated after the dog is found guilty of being vicious. Most states merely find the owner guilty of ownership of a vicious dog. So in New Jersey it would be necessary to establish the dog's innocence to get him off. Taro's priors had included a deadly attack against another pet dog. As a second biter, he was deemed guilty of being vicious and was sentenced to death. His owner appealed. He lost. He then appealed to the Supreme Court of New Jersey. While awaiting appeal, the owner requested a pardon from the governor. The governor, Jim Florio, did not rule because he was leaving office. When the new governor, Christy Whitman, took office in January of the following year, she started her term by issuing a pardon of the dog, the first dog pardon in dog law history.

The custom of prosecuting vicious dogs dates from ancient times. In 1993 Jerry and I went to Europe for our belated honeymoon and traveled to Pompeii which had been buried by the eruption of the volcano Vesuvius in the year 79 a.d. On a tour sightseeing in the village I discovered a home with a tile mosaic of a black dog leashed to a stake. The writing on it read, "Cave canem." I asked the tour guide what the plaque meant and was told "Beware of the dog in Latin."

8

Don't Dogs Have a
Constitutional Right to
Bark at Cats?

"Don't dogs have a constitutional right to bark at cats?"

Fran Baylor, a client, asked me that question after her neighbor complained that Fran's dog had been barking. The red-haired, fiftyish woman living in a suburb of San Diego had been charged with "owning a barking dog."

"I feel," she said, "my dog has a foolproof defense in that he was barking at a cat."

Her question prompted me to think hard about a dog's constitutional rights: does a dog have a right to free speech?

Every good dog law defense is based upon creative thinking. It is a matter of taking the usual interpretation of the laws and rearranging them to work for the defense of an animal, and this is what I try to do in every case.

Nevertheless, there is a problem that makes it difficult to state that a dog barks because he's a dog, and that's what dogs do. The defense centers on whether the barking was such as to constitute a nuisance under the local barking dog statute. If the complaining party believes the dog was a nuisance, the question is whether she or he is being reasonable. Even if the neighbor is found to be unreasonable, there is nothing to keep that person from complaining again the next time the dog barks. If and when this occurs, the dog owner will be forced to defend both her pet and herself again. I felt the best defense to an allegation of a barking dog would be that the complaining party was behaving unreasonably.

One defense which tried my creativity was the case of Tim and Teri Kane. They were in their late twenties and had only been married a year. George, a four-year-old tan Airedale, had been Teri's pet before they were married. "I've never had any complaints about him except from the neighbor who's in the house behind us. His name is Harry Sutton," Teri explained in a plaintive voice.

"In our community all of the yards are separated by six-foot wooden fences. Most of the neighbors have children and dogs, and we all get along," her husband chimed in.

Harry Sutton, the complainant, was in his early forties. His wife was a few years younger and they had a twelve-year-old daughter. Mr. Sutton had called animal control numerous times to complain that George had been barking. The Kanes were charged with "ownership of a barking dog," a crime that carried a penalty of a fine and the possibility of having to get rid of the dog. They hired me to defend them and, of course, George.

Driving over to their neighborhood, I decided to look around and talk to the neighbors. I learned some incredible things about the complaining party. The first person I spoke to was Geri Monahue, the soft-spoken, graying woman who lived next door.

"I'm the attorney representing the Kanes in their barking dog case. Do you know Mr. Sutton?" I asked as she planted carnations in her front yard.

"Oh yes," she replied. "Come inside and I'll tell you. It's not safe to talk out here."

I followed the woman into her home where she proceeded to pour her heart out.

"We bought the house before we knew about the Suttons. The people who lived here before us moved because he drove them crazy. He called the police on our daughters."

"What did your daughters do?"

"They are only six and eight years old," she explained, "and he called the police because they had crossed his front yard coming home from school one day. That's not all. He spies on us when we are in the backyard and watches every car that parks around here."

"What was the name of the people who lived here before you?" I wanted to interview them as possible witnesses.

"Berger," she answered. "Here's their number. They didn't tell us about him before we bought the house. But after we had problems we called them. They admitted that he was what caused them to move. Apparently, he continuously called the police on their teenage sons who worked on their cars in the garage and parked friends' cars out in front of the house."

"Who else is familiar with the Suttons?" I asked.

"Go talk to the Pearsons," she suggested. "They live next door to the Kanes."

"Will you be available to testify on behalf of the Kanes at trial?" I questioned her.

"I certainly will," Geri Monahue responded. "I try to mind my own business, but he's a real nuisance."

Thanking her, I left and went to talk to the Pearsons.

The Pearsons lived in a yellow brick house notable for its green shutters. I barely got to introduce myself when Mrs. Pearson began her story.

"One time," she said, "we saw Mr. Sutton out there." She pointed to the median strip in the boulevard. Making a circular gesture near the side of her head, she added, "He was attempting to catch the leaves falling from the trees before they hit the ground. When I asked him why he was doing that, he said that he had to protect the lawn."

After securing her and her husband as witnesses I walked from house to house lining up other witnesses to Mr. Sutton's obsessive-compulsive behavior. If we could prove he was unreasonable, then a law based upon "reasonableness" would not be established by his opinion.

When I'd finished canvassing the houses, I got in my car and tried to reach Mrs. Berger. "I was given your name by Mrs. Monahue in your old neighborhood. She says you moved because of your neighbor's eccentric behavior. The Kanes are being taken to court because of Mr. Sutton's complaint that their dog barks too much. Would you be willing to testify?"

"We would love to," she responded. "The only reason we left that neighborhood was that nutty man."

Ultimately I found I had eighteen witnesses from the neighborhood who would testify on behalf of the Kanes as to Mr. Sutton's unreasonableness. I knew by then that the prosecutor's only witnesses were Mr. and Mrs. Sutton. The case had been set for night court, and trial was scheduled to begin at 6:00 p.m. that Tuesday. The trial was set to be heard by a judge instead of a jury.

I was seated at the defense table along with Tim and Teri Kane. The district attorney and an assistant were seated at the table for the prosecution. The Suttons and their daughter sat immediately behind them. Behind us sat eighteen witnesses, their spouses and children. Our side of the courtroom was packed. Theirs was empty.

Judge Allan entered the courtroom and everyone stood.

"Good evening, everyone," Judge Allan addressed the courtroom, seeming surprised at the number of people in attendance for a barking dog trial. "I would like to wrap this case up tonight, so let's get started. Are there any preliminary motions?" he asked the attorneys.

"Yes, Your Honor," the prosecutor, Hal Davis, began in his usual tongue-in-cheek manner. "We move to have all of the witnesses sequestered." He did not want any of our witnesses getting ideas from each other's testimony. Since there were so many of our witnesses and only two of theirs, he also didn't want the "gang" effect to intimidate his clients. Because the motion was reasonable and I didn't see any way we could in good faith argue otherwise, we consented. The witnesses were asked to leave the courtroom.

The district attorney rose. "I call Harry Sutton as my first witness.

"Mr. Sutton," Hal Davis said, "please explain the basis for your complaint."

"I live behind the Kanes. They own a tan Airedale that barks all the time." He spoke out of the corner of his mouth as though he had something caught in his tooth that he was trying to wrestle free while he explained the problem. "I have called animal control, but they never seem to do anything, so here we are."

"How often does the dog bark?" The prosecutor's face was a model of seriousness.

"Well, let me explain," Mr. Sutton replied, his eyes glassy. "I have been keeping a log of the dog's barking. I began this log over two years ago and it records every time the dog has barked."

"Is this the log?" the prosecutor asked, knowing the answer.

"Yes, it is."

The prosecutor handed me a copy. I scanned the page and had to suppress a smile. It really did record every time George had barked to the minute for more than two years:

August 2

6:02 a.m.	Started barking
6:03	Stopped barking
6:45	Started barking
6:45	Stopped barking
7:15	Started barking
7:17	Stopped barking
11:52	Started barking
11:53	Stopped barking
1:04 p.m.	Started barking
1:06	Stopped barking

As I considered the complainant's compulsive note-taking, I remembered Mrs. Pearson's crazy gesture. As with the co-ownership contract from the Yale Law School graduate, evidence can sometimes be too good. I handed my copy of the log to the Kanes to review. I returned to listening to Mr. Sutton explain how much the dog barked while the Kanes flipped through the pages of the log.

Turning to Mr. Sutton, I asked, "Why did you keep a log of the dog's barking?"

"Because I knew I would need evidence for this case," he replied.

"And how is it that you are available all day and night to keep this log?" I asked, keeping my tone even.

"If I am unavailable, then my wife and daughter have been instructed to keep the log."

"Do you think there may have been times when the dog barked and you weren't available to record it in your log?" I asked, trying to discredit the accuracy of the log.

"No," he answered. "One of us is always there."

Mr. Sutton was obviously not going to allow me to cast any doubt on the accuracy of his log, and I decided to let his words go for the moment. I made a mental note to go back to this aspect when I had a few moments to question my client.

However, at least I had shown the judge how unusual this man was. All I needed to show was that he was not reasonable, and therefore a law based upon a reasonable disturbance was not going to apply. I felt my witnesses would establish that.

The next witness called to the stand was Mrs. Sutton. Mrs. Sutton restated everything her husband had said.

I conferred with the Kanes who pointed out specific dates in the log when they had been out of town and the dog had been staying at Tim Kane's father's house twenty miles away.

I began to formulate our defense with my only question on cross-examination: "Mrs. Sutton, didn't you consider it unreasonable to do what your husband was asking of you?"

"No," she replied in his defense. "It was not unreasonable for him."

I thought it a novel way to answer and was very sure that as stated it was very true. I had planted the concept in the judge's mind. After all eighteen of our witnesses had been permitted to testify, I called Tim Kane to the stand.

"Mr. Kane, have you had a chance to review Mr. Sutton's log?"

"Yes, I have," he responded.

"Did you find any discrepancies in the log?" I questioned him, knowing the answer.

"Yes, I did," he stated. "The log indicates that my dog was barking on June twenty-first, twenty-second, twenty-third and twenty-fifth. But I know that is not possible."

"And why is that?" I asked, hardly able to contain myself knowing what his response would be.

"Because my wife and I were married on June twenty-first. We immediately left on our honeymoon for a week in the Virgin Islands, and George, our dog, went to stay with my father in Denver."

Now we had impeached the log. The careful records of the Suttons which indicated that they had never missed a single bark were destroyed in credibility because they had recorded barks that could not have been from my client's dog.

"I feel we have established that the Suttons are unreasonably obsessed with George's barking. I believe we have successfully impeached the log, casting doubt on its accuracy. I believe the support of the neighbors has established that Mr. Sutton is prone to unreasonable complaining," I said on summation.

After closing arguments, the judge took the matter into consideration. All of the witnesses were still in the courtroom when, after 11:00 p.m., the judge returned with the verdict.

"Although I think it is clear that Mr. Sutton has exhibited eccentric and unreasonable behavior," the judge said, addressing the packed courtroom, "the same cannot be said for his wife. Even though the log may not be entirely accurate as to entries, there only need to be sufficient entries to establish that the dog has barked enough to cause a nuisance. Therefore, I rule the defendants guilty of ownership of a barking dog."

"Your Honor!" I jumped up as everyone in the courtroom began to grumble. "We move for a motion prohibiting animal control from accepting any future complaints from this man. Without such a ruling, my clients may be back in court every time Mr. Sutton records a bark on his log."

It was clear that the judge sympathized with my clients. But the law as written would not permit him to find them not guilty.

"Motion granted," he responded decisively.

Even though the Kanes had been found guilty, they were not fined and their dog was permitted to stay on the property. Best of all, Mr. Sutton was prevented from filing any more complaints. I didn't think Mrs. Sutton would complain on her own. Essentially we had won, even though the verdict had been "guilty."

A few months later I received another dog barking case.

Annie and Mike Green, a thirtyish couple owned nine sled dogs. All of the dogs were husky mixes except for one old black Labrador who was dying of cancer. But the Lab was kept inside most of the time. By the time they came to my office the barking dog complaints had taken a toll on the couple.

"I'm so afraid that I'll be ordered to get rid of the dogs," Annie said, "that I sleep in the living room near the outside door." At the slightest noise from the dogs she would run outside to quiet them down.

"I'm at a loss," Mike said, patting his wife's plump hand. "At a loss as to what to do to protect my wife. She loves the dogs and loves sled racing and lives in constant fear that they'll be taken from her."

I began to formulate a defense in my mind. Besides the argument of reasonableness, I planned to also concentrate on the burden of proof of the prosecution in establishing that the dogs were barking in the first place. I didn't think most complaining parties would have logs like the Suttons had.

"Where are the dogs kept during the day?" I questioned them.

"Behind the house," Mike answered. "Sled dogs like to have their own doghouses so we have each dog tied to a separate house."

"How do you know that the dogs aren't barking all day?" With nine dogs, it would only take one dog barking to render a guilty verdict.

"Because they are debarked," Annie replied. "We have been so worried about the dogs barking disturbing the neighbors that we have had all the dogs debarked."

"When did you debark the dogs?" I questioned. This wasn't making sense that they had been charged with barking dog for dogs that had been debarked. This case was getting stranger and stranger.

"Right after the first barking dog complaint came in about six months ago."

"The first complaint?" I was curious. "How many times have you been charged with barking dog?"

"Eleven counts in three separate complaints," Mike answered.

This was beginning to look unusual. Why would the district attorney keep filing charges against the same people without permitting them to correct the problem? And how could he file charges against dogs which had been debarked? There had to be more to this.

"Tell me about the earlier charges," I said.

"The first complaint came in last summer. The neighbor across the field from us had complained that our dogs were barking after we left for work," Mike informed me.

"What happened at arraignment?" I asked.

"We pled no contest and agreed to have the dogs debarked. At that time we thought they really might be barking, but now we are not so sure," Mike said.

"Then what happened?" I questioned him.

"About two months later, the same people, the Sampsons, filed another complaint. Animal control came out to the house and observed the dogs. The officer was told that they had all been debarked. We showed her the medical records and she agreed not to file charges. About three days later, we received anonymous phone calls and hang ups.

Annie started getting real fearful that someone would hurt the dogs so that's when she started sleeping downstairs at night. They never barked. Even if they had, it would have been a real hoarse bark."

I shook my head, perplexed. "Then, when were you charged with the next complaint?"

"About a week later animal control came back out and left a complaint."

"Who filed it?"

"The DeBrinneys," Mike answered. "They live next door to the Sampsons. They have a black Labrador named Mickey. He's always running at large. He runs in our yards and gets the dogs going and then they file complaints about our dogs barking. What about their dog running at large?" Mike asked in frustration.

I could understand their frustration, but I had to determine if their dogs were really such a nuisance, or if there were other motives for the neighbors' complaints.

"What is your relationship with the Sampsons and DeBrinneys?"

"We used to get along great," Mike answered. "But last summer the Sampsons wanted to block off an access road that came into the community adjacent to their property. In the winter that road is the only way we can get out of our property without having to drive all the way across the back of the mountain. So we objected."

"So it all started with a neighborhood dispute." That caused the complaints to make sense. There was always more to a barking dog complaint than a barking dog. Once again, I would have to be able to cast doubt on the prosecution's evidence that the dogs had been barking. The fact that they were debarked certainly helped, but even nine debarked dogs barking simultaneously might constitute a barking dog nuisance. I didn't want to test the limits of what is barking with these clients. They had too much to lose.

Suddenly "Pet Detective" had become a recognized career. Clients seemed pleased to know that I had my own pet detective to assist in their cases.

I spoke to Jerry. "I have a client with nine sled dogs. They have been charged with barking dog."

"No doubt," he replied sarcastically.

"What do you mean?" I questioned him.

"Well, they have nine sled dogs. That's what sled dogs do. They bark." Sometimes Jerry's preset determinations of a case were frustrating. But his knowledge of dogs certainly helped.

"But in this case they are debarked," I told him.

"Oh, then that makes it a little more interesting, doesn't it? What is your theory of defense?"

"I think there is some neighborhood dispute going on. Something about an access road into the community that some neighbors want and others don't. There may also be disputes about dogs at large causing the sled dogs to bark. But my big question for you is, how can we show that the dogs don't bark, or if they do, that the barks are too hoarse to be heard across the properties?"

"It's easy to prove that a dog does bark. You can just tape record it or keep a log of the barking. But proving a dog does not bark is going to be a little more difficult. I'll check it out," Jerry told me.

In the meantime I pulled my clients' criminal records. They were right. They had eleven counts of barking dog in the past six months. The first three counts had been dismissed after they pleaded no contest. The district attorney in each of the cases had been the same man, a Mr. Luke Font. It seemed that he was out to hang my clients. The next eight charges were suspended after they had paid a fine. If they were convicted of another charge of barking dog within one year, the eight prior counts would be charged against them. Therefore a guilty verdict of even one count of barking dog would result in my clients being guilty of at least nine counts, and possibly even eleven separate counts. The maximum fine per count was $300. But the worse consequence was that they would probably be ordered to get rid of the dogs. I knew this would destroy Annie, and probably cause a lot of friction between Annie and Mike. I needed to get them off of this charge and this web of complaints that had caught them. Since I had taken on their case another complaint had been filed with animal control and they were facing a twelfth count even if the complaint I was defending them on was dismissed. There was nothing to stop future complaints from coming in even if we were successful at trial. This was like a plague that just kept coming. I had to put an end to the entire issue, not just the matter at hand. I couldn't understand why Mr. Font was so persistent in prosecuting the Greens. Most district attorneys would have resolved this dispute by now.

"What did you find out?" I asked Jerry over dinner two nights later.

"The Sampsons are a real nice family," he answered. I hated it when he made friends with the "other side." "But they do not like the Greens. You were right about them being upset about the road issue. But the DeBrinneys are another story. They have two teenage kids. I think it is the kids who were making the hang up phone calls to the Greens' house. I also pulled the animal control records for the neighborhood. Look at this." He showed me a computer printout of all of the calls to animal control from the Greens' neighborhood since the summer before. There were hundreds of entries.

The Greens had complained about the DeBrinneys' dog at large. The Sampsons complained about the Greens' barking dogs. The DeBrinneys complained about the Sampsons and on and on and on.

"This is quite a neighborhood," I sighed.

"Yeah," Jerry said. "But look here." He pointed out the times for each of the complaints against the Greens for barking dog. All of them were between 7:00 a.m. and 8:00 a.m. on weekday mornings.

"I'll be willing to bet," he continued, "that the DeBrinney kids don't go to school until eight a.m."

"And their parents probably leave before seven a.m.," I concluded for him.

"Exactly," Jerry replied. "I'll find out. But this week I would like to set up surveillance at the house."

"Let's do it," I replied, anxious to get some incriminating evidence. The following day we went to the Greens' home and set a video camera in the upstairs bedroom. From that angle, the camera could observe all of the dogs in the yard. It had a time/date stamp on each frame of the picture and could be preprogrammed to turn on at 7:00 a.m. Not wanting to miss anything, we decided to let it run all day. Each morning a new tape would be put in the camera. After the first week the Greens came to my office with all of their tapes.

"Here they are," Mike told me. "But they are really boring."

I put the first tape into the VCR in my office. Annie, Mike, Jerry and I all pulled up chairs for the exciting viewing of "A Day in the Life of the Greens' Dogs." The day began with the dogs sleeping. Once in a while they would get up and interact, play a little, take some water, but mainly they slept. What they didn't do was bark. After fast forwarding through the tapes, we had a pretty good idea of how the dogs spent their day. But being able to prove they did not bark for five days in a row did not disprove that they had barked on the day of the complaint. We needed to keep taping. The tapes were erased and prepped for another week of taping. Trial was only four weeks away, and we needed our evidence quickly.

"Jerry." I had an idea. "Why don't you interview the DeBrinney kids this week? It might prompt them to take some action."

Jerry and I were beginning to have that silent communication couples who are in synch find. Without saying it, he knew what I meant. Maybe the kids had gotten bored with calling animal control. If he could refresh their memories that there was still a trial pending, they might resume their old activities. If a complaint came in for a barking dog and we could prove they weren't barking, we would have our impeaching evidence.

The next morning around nine he came by my office. "Guess what? I scoped the DeBrinneys' house this morning. The father leaves for work around six-thirty a.m. The mother then leaves about seven. The boy doesn't leave until eight. I spoke to him as he was walking to the school bus, but he wouldn't talk to me. I never saw their daughter."

Our theory that the kids were filing the complaints was looking more and more likely. I called the district attorney, Luke Font, and asked for the best plea prior to trial.

"No plea short of you agreeing to get rid of the dogs," he said.

"That's out of the question," I replied. "So we take the case to trial."

I knew he thought I was bluffing. But not only was I going to take this case to trial, I requested a jury trial. I was going to be sure this matter was resolved now. I did not want the Greens to win at trial only to face future complaints for barking dog. I was not going to let the Sampsons and the DeBrinneys use the criminal justice system to run my clients ragged and broke.

Annie was still sleeping in the living room. If the dogs even began to whine outside, she'd run out and calm them. She wasn't getting much sleep. The stress level in their home was very high. But there were some additional stressful measures I had to inflict on them if the truth were to come out. I told Mike to tape the dogs on the recorder on a daily basis. Then even though I knew another complaint would upset them, I explained that was just what we needed. With only days before trial, we got it. Animal control received another call about a barking dog at the Greens' home. The call came in at ten minutes to 8:00 a.m. on Thursday. I called Mike Green and told him to bring me Thursday morning's tape. We reviewed it together. From 7:00 a.m. to 8:00 a.m. the dogs had been sleeping. There had not been one bark from the group. We had our impeaching evidence.

The trial began the following Thursday at 8:00 a.m. We had not called any witnesses. We planned to present our evidence through the cross-examination of their witnesses and the presentation of the tape. The first step was to impanel a jury. It was important to get jurors who would take the issues seriously. If they didn't think it was important for the Greens to keep their dogs, they wouldn't give the issues serious enough consideration. I had to keep in mind that these people were missing work or being with their families in order to serve as jurors; so I had to respect them as they had to respect my position. Nonetheless, I knew there would be some resentment about being in court for a dog case. I wanted to be sure they understood that they were there because the district attorney had chosen to prosecute this case. It was not my clients' fault that the case had gone to trial and the jurors couldn't be led to believe that it was.

District Attorney Font began the questioning of the prospective jurors. Font, at only about five-foot tall, looked like Michael J. Fox appearing on *L.A. Law*. But I could tell from the brusque greeting he gave me and his serious demeanor he was determined to make a point of this case. It was the first time he had been forced to try a barking dog case, and he wasn't pleased. He was of the opinion that a person charged with barking dog should plead guilty, get rid of the dogs, but certainly not force him to prove that their dogs had been barking. But I was equally determined that my clients would get their day in court, or three days if that was what it was going to take.

Font asked the prospective jurors, "Do any of you object to being here to hear a barking dog case?" There was sarcasm in his voice. He wanted to plant the idea of resentment in the jurors' minds. None of them raised their hands. They were taking their duty seriously. I was pleased.

His next question was, "Have any of you been charged with a dog law violation?"

He wanted to get rid of any sympathetic jurors. One balding man raised his hand and proceeded to explain how his dog had bitten once. Font and I had charts indicating each juror's seat. I starred that juror's seat knowing he would be favorable to our side. But I knew Font was crossing him off his list at the same time. Each attorney can excuse three jurors from the nineteen people that are in the courtroom, leaving a panel of thirteen, twelve active and one alternate juror.

Mr. Font asked a few more questions and then it was my turn.

"Do any of you own cats?" I questioned them, getting a feel for who they were. "And dogs?" Each of the dog owners I starred on my chart. "Do you prefer reading or television?" Although almost all jurors will say they are readers and not television watchers, the question is a good way to get to know the jurors without having any impact on how they will rule. It helps to know what the jurors are like when you're addressing them all day long. I crossed off an older man in a suit. He was a businessman, and I thought he would be resentful at having to spend the day listening to a dog case. He'd probably take that out on the Greens and their nine dogs. I also removed a woman who was a reader with two cats. I thought she would be too sympathetic to anyone who complained about barking dogs. Lastly, I removed a very serious and studious elderly woman whom I felt would view the neighborhood dispute as petty. I needed young dog owners whom I felt could relate to being set up.

Font removed the prospective juror dog owner who had been charged with vicious dog. He removed another young man who owned three dogs and drove a hauling truck, and a young female college student. We now had our jury.

Judge Harold McKenna had a glint in his blue eyes but his tone was very serious as he proceeded to speak to the jurors as a group. "You are here today as jurors in this trial in which the defendants have been charged with three counts (the other counts were not at issue at this trial) of barking dog. If for any reason you feel you can't remain impartial in your determination of the defendant's guilt or innocence, please raise your hand."

None of the jurors responded, but I noticed they listened intently to what the judge was instructing them. I felt we had a good selection of the community who were going to take their jobs as jurors seriously and give the case the respect it deserved.

After his opening statement Font called his first witness.

"I call to the stand Mr. William DeBrinney."

Mr. DeBrinney took the stand and was sworn in. He was tall and dark, dressed in a business suit, and wore the old-fashioned kind of aviator glasses now out of style.

"Mr. DeBrinney," Font began. "I understand you are taking time off from work so we will make this as quick as possible." He was reinforcing the "waste of time" idea in the jury's mind again. I was going to be sure he didn't get away with it.

"Did you file a complaint on September twentieth about the Greens' dogs?"

"Yes, I did," he said in a clipped voice.

"What did you state in your complaint?"

"That their dogs had been barking." He enunciated each syllable. I wondered if he'd had speech lessons.

"How long had they been barking?"

"I'm not sure that day." He paused and then looked at the jurors. "They are always barking."

"Objection," I interrupted. "Irrelevant. Only the counts at hand are at issue."

"Sustained," the judge agreed. "Limit your response to this time, Mr. DeBrinney," the judge addressed the witness. But I bit my lip. The damage had been done: the jurors had been told the dogs barked all of the time.

"On this occasion," Font said, emphasizing the word occasion, "how long were they barking for?"

Maybe they were on the same debating team, I thought.

"I'm not sure." Mr. DeBrinney hesitated. "I think about a half hour or so."

He wasn't sure because I was sure he had not been home when the complaint had been filed. On cross-examination, I asked him, "Mr. DeBrinney, where do you work?"

"At Reliable." He named an insurance company.

"And what time do you leave for work in the mornings?"

"Usually before seven a.m.," he replied.

"The complaint called into animal control on September twentieth came in at eight-oh-five a.m. Would you have been home at that time?"

"I'm not sure which day was which." He started to cover his tracks. "Some days my son or daughter may have called in, but I was aware of the dogs barking."

"Did you ever call animal control yourself?" I asked him.

He thought for a minute. "I don't think I ever actually filed the complaint. But I was aware that the dogs were barking."

"If you didn't call animal control on September twentieth, who did?"

"Probably Julie or Bill, my kids."

We had been right and Mr. DeBrinney had been honest enough to admit it. His testimony was no longer relevant. Font had needed him to testify because he was more credible than his children.

Font next called Julie DeBrinney to the stand. She was a nineteen-year-old college student with tricolored hair and multi earrings. I bet that style drives her father crazy, I thought, looking at her.

"Julie," Font began, "did you call animal control on September twentieth?"

"Yes."

"Why?"

"Because the Greens' dogs had been barking."

"How long had they been barking for?"

"At least an hour." She had been outside of the court-room during her father's testimony and could not match notes with his testimony.

I stood up to begin my cross-examination and the Judge interrupted me. "I have received a request from Mr. DeBrinney to return to work, Ms. Cawley," he addressed me. "Do you need Mr. DeBrinney any longer?"

I looked over at DeBrinney. I knew he wanted to get back to his job. But the Greens and all of the jurors were going to have to stay to the end, and I was not about to let him off that easy.

"Yes, Your Honor," I replied. "I may need to recall him after I hear the testimony of his children and neighbors." Which was true. After all, the district attorney had called all of these witnesses, not me. I wasn't going to let a single one go home early. If they wanted to prove that the Greens' dogs were a nuisance they would have to stay for the duration of the trial. The Greens had suffered through this charade for more than six months. The complaining parties were going to have to suffer with them for a couple of days.

While Mr. DeBrinney and the rest of the witnesses waited in the hallway of the courthouse, I cross-examined

Julie DeBrinney.

"Julie, aren't you in college?"

"Yes," she answered in a snippy manner. She didn't like me and she was going to show how cool she was in giving me all the right answers.

"Where are you in school?" I continued.

"At Colorado Union."

The college was about ten hours out of Denver.

"Well, shouldn't you have been in school on September twentieth?" I challenged her.

"I'm taking this semester off." I'm sure there was a good story behind that but it was irrelevant here. She was getting cautious of me now and careful in giving her answers. I knew I had the right person.

"What day of the week was September twentieth?" I asked, having already ascertained it had been a Tuesday.

"How should I know?" she snapped. "That was over six months ago."

I looked over at the jury appraisingly. They were not warming to her bitchy attitude. I kept on drilling to get her more and more angry with me. I needed the jury to know her character. It didn't take long.

"Don't you have a dog yourself?"

"No."

"No?" I questioned, raising my voice in doubt. "Have you ever heard of a Labrador that resides at twelve sixty-three Wild River Drive?"

"It's not my dog. It's my family's dog," she snapped.

"Oh." I nodded my head as though she had clarified a very confusing issue, when I knew all she had done was convince the jury that she was a rebellious teen with an attitude.

"Do you know whether your parents were charged with dog at large because of Mickey having been at large on the weekend of September eighteenth?"

"Yes."

"Yes, you know?" I kept my voice level.

"Yes."

"Were they charged?"

"Yes."

"And do you know who called animal control because of Mickey's running at large?"

"Yes."

"Who?"

"The Greens."

"Did that upset you?" Her attitude was breaking.

"Yes," she said defiantly.

"You were upset because the Greens had called animal control on Mickey, and you called animal control on the Greens to get revenge, didn't you?"

She obviously hadn't been expecting my point. She burst into tears. Obviously, what had started as a phone call out of spite had turned into a very serious situation and now it was out in the open and she was getting scared. I didn't want her to become too teary or she might start getting the sympathy of the jury.

"No," she nearly whispered. But her answer didn't matter. The jury knew what had happened.

"That's my last question," I said. "You may be excused."

"Ms. Cawley," Judge McKenna addressed me. "Will you be needing Ms. DeBrinney? I understand she has a job to return to." He asked the question, but he already knew the answer. He knew exactly what I was up to.

"Yes, Your Honor," I replied. "I may need to recall her." She was going to have to wait in the hallway with the rest of the witnesses. The longer she sat there, the less likely she was to call animal control on the Greens again.

By now it was nearly noon. The judge decided to break for lunch. The witnesses were permitted to go to lunch but not leave. After I returned from lunch with the Greens who looked less anxious than they had in six months, I was told that Judge McKenna wanted to see me in his chambers.

When I arrived in the judge's chambers, Luke Font was already there. He was standing against the wall as the tall, lanky judge reclined in his desk chair. I took a seat across from the judge.

"I understand that this is an important matter to your clients, Ms. Cawley," he began. "But I have a full calendar. Don't you please think we could wrap this up any quicker than this?"

"What do you mean, Your Honor?" What was behind his words? That I should throw in the towel and have them admit their guilt?

"I mean," he persisted, "couldn't you find a plea to accept?" It was plain the judge felt that dog problems didn't belong in court, especially his court. But, if the system didn't want dog cases to be tried in courtrooms, then dog laws shouldn't be criminal. Every criminal defendant deserves the best defense possible, and my clients were not going to be blamed for seeking such justice.

"But, Your Honor," I replied softly, "we have never been offered a plea."

I looked at the judge. His face was bright red. I thought

the judge was going to blow. He spun in his chair and glared at Font.

"You haven't offered her a plea?" he shouted. Font turned away and shrugged his shoulders. "Offer her one! Now!" McKenna ordered, pointing at us to get out. We quickly scampered out of the judge's chambers. It had been clear that McKenna was not going to permit this trial to continue. Whoever forced it to continue was going to be in trouble with this judge. It was Font's fault we were here, and he knew it. Moreover, as a district attorney he appeared before this judge more often than I did and had much more to lose.

"How about you plead to one count of dog barking?" Font suggested when we reached the hallway.

"It doesn't matter if it's one count or three. You know these people have eleven counts on them. More come in every day. This has got to stop. We will not take any pleas to barking dog but we will plead to a lesser offense," I said, holding my ground.

Now, courthouse law does not always proceed by the book or by any preconceived abstract doctrine about justice. Therefore, in criminal court it's possible to assign one crime to a defendant even though everyone knows the defendant did not commit that crime. This is done because it is a lesser charge than the one pending against the defendant. For example, a speeding ticket with points can be reduced to a headlight broken, even though the headlight might be in perfect working order. It is a quirk of the criminal justice system.

"Like what?" he questioned suspiciously.

"Like failure to license." I suggested a criminal dog law that carried a ten-dollar fine and had no consequences because once the dog was licensed the charge was dropped.

"Oh jeez," he sputtered and spun away in disgust and frustration.

"Okay," I answered. "Let's continue the trial." Font knew that his twelve witnesses were just coming back from lunch. He also knew that the witnesses who had not yet testified were aware they would not be permitted to go home until the entire trial was over, which could be a fairly long time—even overnight.

I began to walk away.

"No." He stopped me. "What kind of plea do you want?"

Now I had him.

"I want one count of failure to license and a ruling that you accept no more complaints from that neighborhood about the Greens' dogs."

He pursed his lips, looking like he was eating a sock.

"Okay," he consented grudgingly.

The Greens accepted a plea to one count of failure to license. Their ordeal had ended. I didn't think Julie DeBrinney would be calling animal control on anyone in the near future.

Everything had worked out for the best for my clients, but the district attorney was not soon to forget his embarrassment on this one. When we met again months later in a vicious dog trial, he sought revenge by taking to trial a case where he was sure he would win against me. But he didn't.

Even though the court system can work with proper perseverance, I have always believed that the best resolution to barking dog cases is to have the dog owner and the complaining person work out an agreement. Otherwise, even though one case is resolved, later a new complaint gets filed and it starts all over again.

Although the Green trial had been successful, with Lynn Martin, the next person to come to me with a barking dog complaint filed against them, I suggested mediation between the parties. I recommended that Lynn, a single working woman with two mixed breed dogs, get together with her next door neighbor, Sydney Lewis, a college student. Lynn left her house at 7:00 a.m. each morning leaving her two dogs, nine-year-old Buster and two-year-old Chelsea, in the backyard. She returned home around six and let the dogs back in. Sydney had no classes until noon. She liked to sleep until ten or eleven. The dogs' barking wouldn't permit this; so she filed a complaint. The two agreed to arbitration rather than face a lengthy trial. I agreed to assist Lynn in the arbitration.

The arbitration was held on the campus of the University of Denver College of Law and was sponsored by the law school's dispute resolution class. There was no cost to either party. If a successful resolution was worked out, the city attorney for Denver—where I was still batting a thousand in dismissals—had agreed to dismiss all charges against Lynn. The law students were very hopeful that a resolution could be worked out as they began the negotiations.

First, Sydney told about all of the barking by Buster and Chelsea. Then they discussed possible solutions. The law students went through every possible scenario to set up a situation that would accommodate the needs of both Lynn and Sydney. To the students' and the two adversaries' credit, they persevered for nearly six hours of negotiation. By the end of the night I was bone tired and had learned that arbitration took just as long as a trial. But finally a resolution was determined. It was agreed that Lynn would keep the dogs inside when she went to work and Sydney would have a key to Lynn's house. When Sydney got up, she would go over and let Buster and Chelsea out. It had taken six hours of tiring negotiation for the two women to trust each other enough to come up with such a simple solution. But, on the other hand, arbitration had worked and the charges against Lynn were dismissed. When I saw her a year later, it was still working.

Matters like dogs barking seem inconsequential to some but, for the dog lover who may have to get rid of a beloved pet, there is more than inconvenience at stake. And for the person unable to function or being kept awake by a barking animal, sanity may be.

Whether a case is taken to trial or arbitration, some resolution to the barking dog problem must be had in order for neighbors to live at peace.

9

The Riot Act

It was ten degrees below zero on a February night when I received a frantic telephone call from Glen Sutter. "I'm worried sick about my poor dog and her puppy," he said.

"Maybe you'd better explain," I replied.

He began, "I had an agreement to breed my female Newfoundland, Bary, with Shari Wright's male dog, Star. We agreed that the breeding would take place at Shari's place and when it was time for the puppies to be born, that would be at Shari's place as well. I took Bary over there last week when she was scheduled to deliver, and the puppy was born by Cesarean section on January tenth. The next day Shari called me at work and told me, 'Come get your dog.' Tonight I had to go get Bary. Shari had left her alone in the back of her truck in the dark, and there was no puppy. She refuses to turn over the puppy to me."

The thought of the poor mother dog alone in a crate in the cold while her six-day-old puppy was locked inside upset me. How could anyone who considered themselves a breeder permit a mother to be separated from her young pup?

"How is your dog doing?" I questioned him.

"She is in good health, but she misses the puppy. She wanders the house looking for him. I just have to get him back for her," he told me insistently. "I have to."

I was very concerned for the puppy, the mother, and the owner. I agreed to take the case. "Please fax me the breeding agreement and all the other relevant information," I instructed.

The next morning I had all the documents I needed. The original agreement provided that Glen would offer the services of his dog, Bary; Shari would offer the stud services of her dog, Star. When the puppies were born, Glen would get first pick of the litter, Shari second, and they would alternate selections until all of the puppies were accounted for. What they had not accounted for was that there would only be one live puppy born. Another female puppy had been stillborn.

Because of the puppy's young age, I wanted to move quickly to reunite him with the mother. I agreed to visit Glen at his home that evening. His home was located a few miles into the foothills on a dark dirt road which made driving difficult. It looked like the classic western badlands. Entering the community through a gate, I drove up over a hill to a little wooden house surrounded by grazing land.

Glen met me at the door. He was tall and thin with long sideburns which were gray like his receding hairline. He was very soft-spoken and welcomed me into the home. The house was sparsely furnished. Except for a table in the kitchen with two chairs and a small sofa in the front room, there was no place to sit. I sat on the sofa and Glen on a kitchen chair he pulled up. The temperature in the home was no more than fifty degrees.

"I keep the temperature low in here to keep Bary comfortable," Glen informed me.

"I'm sure she's very comfortable," I hinted. Glen accepted the hint and turned up the heat.

Glen brought Bary, a black and white Newfoundland about five years old, into the room. She immediately came over to check me out and then snuggled up against Glen's leg, lying down at his feet. It was apparent she was really bonded to him. I watched closely. I always need to see how a dog reacts with an owner. It gives me greater insight into the owner than anything the owner might say.

After reviewing the contracts and communications between Glen and Shari about the ownership of the puppy, I said, "I think I can get the puppy back for you."

"I don't know how we can thank you," he said and stroked Bary.

The next day I sent a demand letter to Shari asking for the return of the puppy. For ten days she ignored it. I called her and when she finally spoke to me she threatened to destroy the puppy if we continued. Later, her attorney called me and said they were thinking of a settlement offer. Three more days passed and they made no offer. At that point, I filed a complaint in replevin for the return of the puppy. Because Shari had told me that the puppy would die if we brought legal action against her, I filed an order for immediate possession. It was granted. That night, nearly four weeks after Bary and her puppy had been separated, the sheriff's department went to Shari's home and demanded the return of the puppy. A short while later she turned a dog over to them, and they left. Then they delivered the Newfoundland puppy to Glen. An agitated Glen called me immediately. The puppy they delivered, supposedly only five weeks old, weighed thirty-five pounds. They had delivered the wrong dog.

Because the replevin had taken place on the Friday before Presidents' Day holiday weekend, we could not get back into court until Tuesday, four days later. That morning I filed a motion for contempt of court. Shari and her attorney appeared. In a dog crate was the contested puppy.

When the magistrate who had entered the order which Shari defied entered the courtroom, we all stood. Shari, her attorney, and the five-week-old puppy took their seats at the defense table. I sat at the table for the plaintiff along with Glen and the oversized thirty-five pound black puppy delivered to Glenn, who was not too fond of sitting still in court.

"Judge Harris." I began explaining to the court what had happened to bring us into his courtroom.

He glared at me.

"I do not appreciate your bringing this action into my courtroom." His sonorous voice rose and paused. "I have child abuse cases, and murders, and you are fighting over a puppy when there is a contract that is clear on its face. If that puppy isn't turned over immediately, someone is going to jail." Turning away from me, the judge shouted from the bench at Shari and her attorney. Shari began to cry.

Then, as if on cue:

The huge thirty-five-pound furry impostor whose leash Glenn held began to bark.

My tiny black and white puppy client imprisoned in his crate started whimpering pitifully.

My human client began to cry.

The attorney for Shari cleared his throat and jumped to his feet to loudly defend his client's ludicrous position, over-turning his chair.

Amid the uproar the judge's gavel crashed down.

"Order in the courtroom," the judge yelled, banging his gavel again. "If that puppy isn't turned over immediately, someone here is going to jail." His eyes glowered at Shari.

Looking around at the chaotic scene, I pressed my hand to my throbbing temple. I thought to myself, *How in the world did I get here?*

"But your Honor," Shari's attorney John Wallace addressed the Court, "My client has acted in good faith."

"By producing the wrong dog to the Sheriff?", the Magistrate questioned Wallace.

"She was scared," Wallace continued while still under the glare of the Court. "The puppy subject of this dispute was not on his property at the time. She was told that she would go to jail if she didn't turn over the dog. So she gave the officer this dog." Wallace pointed to the thirty-five pound puppy that was wrestling himself free of Glen's grip giving the appearance of a rambunctious lion cub rather than a five week-old newborn dog.

The magistrate smiled at the puppy. "I have dogs myself and I don't think any dog owner could in good faith mistake this dog for a five week-old puppy. But you have brought the puppy with you here today so I will not be ruling on the motion for contempt at this time. So long as the puppy is delivered to Mr. Sutter by 5:00 p.m. today, your client should be out of trouble."

"One more thing Judge," Wallace jumped up again, gaining a little confidence now that his client wasn't facing jail time. "The Rule for Motions for Replevin dictates that a bond must be posted before property can be delivered to the moving party. Mr. Sutter never posted bond in this case."

Legally, Wallace was correct. We had not been asked to post bond when we had filed the Motion for Replevin. But in principal, it was a minor infraction in light of the behavior of his client. "Ms. Cawley," the Judge addressed me, "Do you have a dollar?"

"Yes Your Honor, of course."

"Post bond of one dollar on the way out."

"Umm, Your Honor," once again Wallace was on his feet. By now, both puppies had become tired of the proceedings and had fallen asleep. The little one in his crate and the big one at Glen's feet under the Plaintiff's table. Wallace continued, "The plaintiff declares the value of the puppy to be $1500 in his Motion."

"But if the puppy is worth $1500," Wallace proceeded cautiously, knowing he was on shaky ground, "Shouldn't the bond be at least $1500?".

Now the Judge had had enough, his voice was thunderous, "I have ordered bond of one dollar; in this case I think it is appropriate. If you want to file an appeal of this ruling go ahead, but it will take you thirty days just to get the transcript. I don't want this case back in my courtroom. The attorneys need to get together and work out a settlement. If you want me to enter the settlement as a court order, I will do so. So ordered." The Judge banged the gavel and strode from the courtroom.

"Do you have a minute to talk settlement?" Wallace asked me.

"Sure," I responded, "Let's have the clients put the puppies back in their respective vehicles until we are ready to make the exchange." After the puppies were safely ensconced in their crates in the vehicles, Glen, Shari, and Wallace, and I met in a conference room in the courthouse.

I had instructed Glen that no matter what Shari said, and no matter how hard Wallace tried to provoke him, not to say anything. He sat down next to me with his hands crossed. Shari and Wallace sat across the conference table. Shari was still leaking the occasional tear.

Wallace began the conference. "Well, you seem to have beaten us at every move so far. We would like to settle this matter if possible."

I knew there was no way Wallace would ever appear in front of that Judge again on this matter, so I figured we had some pretty heavy leveraging power.

"What do you propose?", I questioned wanting him to assert his position first.

"We will agree that Glen can have the puppy. He can keep the dog and have her signed over to be registered entirely in his name. He must agree to never contact my client or go anywhere near her property. And he must not talk about this case to anyone," Wallace concluded his offer.

Except for his last provision of not talking to anyone, everything else was already agreed to as matter of law. My client had no intention of going near Shari again, but I knew their concern was putting a "gag" order on Glen.

"Who specifically don't you want him to talk to?," I questioned Wallace.

"Other breeders, rescue clubs, and the AKC," he answered.

So that was it. Shari was afraid that Glen would file a complaint against her with the AKC and she would be branded as a "bad breeder." I knew Glen wanted to file the complaint, but only because he thought Shari's behavior in separating the puppy from its mother should be reviewed. However, he would need to communicate with the AKC in the event he needed to register the puppy and Shari would not cooperate with the litter papers.

"So long as your client agrees to sign off on all AKC papers, Bary's and the puppy's, then we can agree to your requests," I replied.

"Okay," Wallace looked surprised, "Then we have a deal?"

I looked to Glen for confirmation and he nodded his agreement, "Yes, but we have one request," I told Wallace, "You prepare the settlement papers."

He knew I was concerned about the escalating fees on my client's behalf. Having to file the Motion for Contempt because of the wrong puppy being delivered was an expensive process for Glen. His client should have delivered the right dog in the first place, or better yet, not have wrongfully taken the puppy at all. We agreed, then Glenn and I left for the parking lot to finally retrieve the right puppy.

My husband Jerry was in the park next to the courthouse playing with the thirty-five pound puppy. Shari came towards us carrying the little puppy. She had a scowl on her face. And daggers in here eyes, We knew something was up. Immediately, I clasped the little pup in my arms, not wanting any hesitation. Shari grabbed the bigger puppy by the scruff of the neck and pitched him into a crate in the back of her car.

Jerry, Glen, and I all watched in shock. The dog hadn't received rough treatment the whole time he had been with Glen and us. I felt a tinge of guilt for permitting the puppy to be returned to Shari, but neither Glen nor I had any legal right to the dog.

We quickly turned our attention to the puppy, which appeared to be a fluff ball with eyes, all black except for a small dab of white on his chest. He began to whimper as I handed him over to Glen. And then, it was as if the small dog knew he had finally found a good home. Within moments, he snuggled peacefully in Glen's arms.

10

"Your Dog Wasn't Worth Anything Anyway"

The most emotional of dog law cases are those of wrongful death. As with people, a wrongful death occurs when a dog dies because of someone's negligence. And, as with the death of a person, the death of a dog can cause great emotional distress. But, unlike human beings, dogs, under the law, have no intrinsic value—except, of course, to those who love them.

The first case for wrongful death that I was able to file in the Federal District Court for the State of Colorado was the one brought to me by Valerie and Larry Stephens. Their family had owned a thirteen-year-old black Labrador retriever named Milo and another small mixed-breed dog named Jojo. "We live in a suburban community with yards behind six-foot wooden privacy fences," Valerie, a plump motherly-looking woman with gray running through her dark curly hair, told me in an emotional voice. "We'd fallen behind in

143

our payments to the Public Service Company," she went on. "After receiving a notice that our service would be disconnected, we called PSC and tried to work out a payment plan. PSC had our work and home phone numbers. They agreed to the plan. After we were late on one payment, PSC sent two men to remove the meter."

Because the meter was the property of the PSC and its placement on the homeowner's property is only done pursuant to an easement permitting the PSC to enter the property to remove it when necessary, the PSC employees were acting legally when they went to remove the meter. When they got to the property, they saw a Beware of the Dog sign on the gate and heard dogs barking in the backyard. Following standard procedure, they called the sheriff's department and requested assistance from animal control to restrain the dog while they entered the property. A few minutes later, Reserve Deputy Sheriff Menton, acting on behalf of animal control, showed up at the property. On his instructions, the three men entered the backyard of the home.

The first PSC employee made it down the driveway and around the house, followed by his coworker, before the dogs came out of the house through an opened door into the backyard. The first dog, Milo, passed the PSC employees and headed directly towards Menton who pulled out his .45 caliber revolver and shot the dog in the head, killing him instantly. The three men then removed the meter and took the dog to Menton's car, leaving a note on the door: "Your dog is dead. Call about the circumstances."

When Valerie Stephens, who had two teenage children and one grandchild, came home from work that day she didn't see the note which had been written on the back of a business card. She couldn't find her dog and became concerned. She called Larry at work and told him the dog was missing and the electricity was off. Being familiar with Public Service's procedures, he told her to look for a message on the front door. She found the note about the dog and became hysterical. Larry rushed home from work, not understanding her garbled tearful explanation. Upon calling the sheriff's department, the family was told, "That is what you get when you don't pay your electric bills."

When the Stephenses came to my office, they said hysterically, "We want to sue everyone involved." I agreed that the sheriff's department had acted improperly.

I called Sheriff Barr and he suggested I come to his office for a meeting. Even though his office was nearly thirty miles south of Denver, I agreed to be there the following afternoon. I thought we would at least get an apology. I was wrong.

"Come in," Sheriff Barr instructed me upon arriving at the county offices.

I said, softly stressing my first word, "You are aware that one of your officers killed my clients' dog in its own backyard."

"Yes," he answered, shrugging. "Would you like some coffee?"

Barr expressed no concern about the matter and acted with such smugness that I immediately disliked him. He was in his early fifties and was dressed in jeans and a western shirt and chewed tobacco the whole time. I realized I was dealing with a person who still felt Colorado was the Old West.

"No, thank you. I would like to discuss the circumstances surrounding the incident in which my clients' dog was killed by Officer Menton."

"Well, I can't discuss that because it is up for Internal Affairs investigation. Do you like dogs?"

Ignoring his question, I stated, "If you can't discuss this matter with me, why did you have me drive all the way down here to meet you?"

"I wanted to meet you," he responded. "Are you sure you wouldn't like some coffee?" he asked again as he poured himself a cup.

"No, thank you." I answered, trying to get him back on the subject at hand. "Your deputy officer fired a .45 caliber gun in my clients' backyard instantly killing their dog and left a note saying, 'Your dog is dead. Please call about the circumstances,' and you won't even discuss this matter with me?"

"We are the county. We have governmental immunity. What are you going to do, sue us?"

I was getting nowhere with this man and he was infuriating me. I had driven thirty miles to meet with him and all he wanted to do was offer me coffee.

"I guess I will have to sue you just to get the answers my clients deserve." I nodded, biting back my irritation at his callousness.

Perfunctorily thanking him for seeing me, I left his office already planning the grounds for the lawsuit. There might be governmental immunity for ordinary negligence, but I didn't believe that this was ordinary negligence. This was extraordinary.

My next stop was my client's house. I had to tell Valerie and Larry that I'd found out nothing from the sheriff and we had no choice but to file suit. They agreed. We then went into the backyard to view where the incident had taken place. The property had a driveway on the right side of the house that was blocked by a six-foot wooden fence with a gate.

"That's where the Beware of the Dog sign was." Larry pointed. The gate was latched and secured by a tied wire. The driveway continued along the right side of the house for about ten feet. The yard, which was all concrete, opened up behind the house. There was an empty swimming pool in the middle of the yard. The house had sliding glass doors which opened up to a patio to the left of the pool. From the right rear corner of the house to the pool there was only about a three-foot wide walkway.

"Let's retrace his steps," I said as Valerie and Larry followed me. "The officer entered the gate and came up the driveway about six feet. He said he then saw the dog come around the corner charging at him, when he reached out and fired." I didn't add that he had also said the dog's body landed about five feet down the driveway.

Observing the yard, I realized there wasn't enough space for the incident to occur the way the officer had described. The dog would have had to come through a three-foot-wide walkway next to the empty pool before the officer could have seen him. The dog had passed the two PSC employees who had gone through the walkway by then, yet the officer claimed the dog had been charging at him. I was now prepared for the deposition of the officer.

Public Service employees didn't need to call the sheriff's department to come and kill the dog. They could have done that. On the other hand, the sheriff's department, that county's animal control, was supposed to be experienced in restraining dogs properly. As expert in animal restraint, the officer had a strong duty of care in handling the dog. I didn't think it would be difficult to prove he had breached that duty of care and acted negligently. I scheduled Menton for a deposition. A week later the officer and his counsel appeared at my office.

After the basic introductory questions, I began. "Why did you go to the property?"

Menton ran his fingers through his crewcut hair. I hoped it was as sticky and sharp as it looked. "I received a call on my radio from headquarters instructing me to go to that property to assist Public Service in the removal of a meter," he said, obviously annoyed at being there.

I noted that and decided to press him quickly. "Were you told there were dogs on the property?"

"Yes."

"What equipment did you take with you to restrain the dogs?"

"I had a sound deterrent and a club."

"And a .45 revolver?"

"Objection," the attorney for the officer piped in. "Argumentative."

"Did you have a .45 revolver with you that day?" I asked, rewording the question.

Menton looked to his attorney for help.

"Go ahead and answer," the attorney, Jed Hines, instructed.

"Yes."

"Did you use the sound deterrent?"

"Yes. When I first entered the property, I sounded the alarm to deter the dog. But it didn't work. He kept coming at me."

Good. He'd made a claim that the facts would prove untrue. I wasn't going to let that go unchallenged, but I moved cautiously.

"How far away was the dog when you first emitted the sound?"

"He had just come around the corner of the house. About six feet, I guess."

"And then what did you do?" I said, keeping my tone even.

"I didn't have time to reach for the club so I grabbed my revolver and shot the dog."

Now I had him. "How far away were you when you shot the dog?"

"About three feet."

I asked a few more questions and then permitted him to leave.

After the deposition of Menton I felt I had a pretty clear picture of what had happened. Menton had emitted the sound deterrent which infuriated an otherwise passive dog. The yard was too congested for Menton to see the dog until he was right in front of him. He reacted and killed the dog.

All I needed was evidence that Menton had acted negligently because of negligence of the sheriff's department in not training him properly, or intentionally in killing Milo. I believed the negligence would be the easier way to go. I then interviewed Director Hugh Tiber of the county animal control.

"Does it seem reasonable that Menton would have emitted the sound deterrent when he couldn't even see the dog?" I asked Tiber.

"Definitely not," he answered. "When a sound deterrent is emitted at a dog in closed quarters, the sound can drive the dog mad because he has no escape. My officers are trained to never use the alarm in a confined area."

"What other means of restraint could the officer have used?" I questioned him.

"We generally recommend a restraining bar." Tiber showed me a short bar with a noose on the end of it. "Once the dog is captured, he cannot get close enough to injure the handler and he can then be controlled."

"Is that what you think should have been used in this instance?" I asked, needing his expert opinion.

"Definitely," he responded to my satisfaction. I needed another opinion as to the use of the gun so I could tie its use back to the negligence of the county in permitting the officer to carry a gun to control pet animals.

"Do you find it unusual that an animal control officer in a suburban neighborhood carries a gun?" I questioned.

"Our officers don't ever carry guns. None of the surrounding communities permit animal control officers to carry guns. I'm really surprised this guy was allowed to carry a gun." I now had my first expert witness. The next day, I had my second one when I received a letter:

Dear Ms. Cawley:

Two years ago I was in police officer training classes with Officer Menton, the officer who killed that black Labrador retriever. Menton was afraid of dogs. He was also trigger-happy Please pull his review files for those classes and they will show that he failed all of his gun classes.

The letter was signed by another police officer who now worked in a neighboring county. I soon received another letter from a local animal control officer who had worked in the same county as Menton. "In that county," the letter stated, "we used to carry high-power rifles for killing wild animals such as mountain lions, bears and coyotes. But about six years ago, when the population boom hit, we were instructed that we could no longer carry the rifles. I seriously doubt that animal control is permitted to carry weapons still." It was signed, "Sincerely, Grant Levin."

Whether or not an animal control officer was permitted to carry a gun or not would determine who the defendants would be. We wanted the county and the sheriff's department to be defendants. If the officer had acted outside the scope of his employment, then the county would not be responsible and our only recourse would be suing Menton. On the other hand, if he acted outside the scope of his employment, they could not present the defense of governmental immunity for the officer.

If Menton had acted with the county's authority and within the scope of his employment, then the county and the sheriff's department would be vicariously liable for his negligent actions. But then they would argue the defense of governmental immunity which deems a governmental agency and its employees immune from liability for their negligent actions. I had to find a way of getting around the governmental immunity argument without losing Menton as a defendant as well.

In the complaint, I charged all three defendants, the county, the sheriff's department, and the officer:

1) Intentional killing of a dog
2) Deprivation of property
3) Negligence
4) Negligent infliction of emotional distress
5) Trespass
6) Trespass to chattels
7) Conversion of property
8) Public nuisance

9) Private nuisance

10) Invasion of privacy

11) Negligent hiring

12) Negligent training

13) Negligent furnishing of firearms, and

14) Negligent failure to terminate

By proving the county and sheriff's department had acted negligently as charged in counts ten through fourteen, I hoped to keep them as defendants even if the officer's actions were found to have been intentional or outside the scope of his employment.

But even if I were to prove liability, I knew I still had to establish damages. Under Colorado law, the maximum that a governmental agency can be sued for was then $400,000. So I claimed $400,000. Proving those damages would be more difficult. Since Colorado did not have a statute permitting punitive damages for outrageous conduct or the intentional destruction of property, I could not find anything for which the clients could recover punitives. Colorado had still not permitted recovery of emotional distress damages for the wrongful death of a dog, but I was hoping that this case might be the case to change that. In order to change the law though, the case would have to be lost at trial level and then successful on appeal, which could be a lengthy and expensive process. Just how expensive my clients learned at the first settlement conference ordered by the district court judge.

When we appeared in chambers, Judge Harlan looked straight at the Stephenses and asked them, "How much money do you have?"

"I beg your pardon," Larry replied.

"I hope you have a lot more money than you did on the day your dog died. You didn't have enough to pay the electric bill, right?"

"That's true," Larry answered.

"But now you have enough money to bring this lawsuit against the county?"

"I have a job now, Your Honor, which plays quite well. I think we will be able to handle the expenses."

Of course the judge was hoping to get the details of our arrangement, but I was happy to see Larry was close-mouthed.

I had taken the case on a contingency basis, so the clients didn't have attorney fees. Nonetheless, the cost of depositions and expert witnesses could certainly be expensive.

"This case could cost you fifty thousand dollars," Judge Harlan told my clients. "Even if you win on the issues of liability, you don't have any damages. I have a black Lab myself. He's a great dog, but we got him at the pound and he only cost us fifty dollars. You don't have the money for this kind of lawsuit. Go buy yourselves another dog."

Unfortunately, my clients were between a rock and a hard place. Once again, the value of a dog was the determining factor. With a judge with that attitude, we had no hope of winning and could only then hope for success on appeal. Because of governmental immunity, we would probably lose the county and sheriff's department as defendants and we would have a $50,000 litigation on appeal against an officer who had no money even if we were successful. I had to recommend that the Stephenses drop the suit. I couldn't afford to litigate to appeal and neither could they. Once again a dog law case was tossed out of the courtroom. Once again the feelings of my childhood against the unfair treatment of animals with no champion to fight for their rights flared. Some day I was going to right these wrongs.

Veterinary malpractice cases are also difficult to fight, because, as with any malpractice case, another expert, a veterinarian, has to testify that his colleague in the profession acted negligently. Very few professionals are willing to do this. Therefore, proving negligence is very hard. It becomes even harder when the veterinarian is an employee of the state, a governmental entity. Such an employee is protected as are diplomats, etc. by governmental immunity.

In one very appalling case, Patti Ritter, a striking brunette, came to my office to tell me about her golden retriever, Katie, who had been taken to a state hospital to be treated for internal complications. Katie underwent surgery. After she returned home, she got sicker and sicker. A week later Patti took her to another veterinarian. An x-ray showed a sixteen-inch long pair of scissors, opened, inside of the dog. The scissors were removed, but the dog died.

A Borzoi had been treated at the same hospital after it had been hit by a car. A second veterinarian told the owner that the medical treatment the dog had received had been negligent, but that if the owner sued the state, the new veterinarian would refuse to treat her dog. I have been called in on other cases against state veterinary hospitals across the country, but the defense of governmental immunity is too strong, and I have had to decline taking these cases to trial even though there may have been strong negligence on the part of the veterinarian. Knowing that owners of dogs who have been injured or die because of the negligence of veterinarians who are unqualified, uncaring or just plain lazy and that these owners do not have a chance of recovery under the law is very frustrating.

I have had some success with veterinary malpractice cases against private veterinarians who have been negligent. Most veterinarians are insured, as are veterinary clinics. Any negligence resulting in an injury to a dog will generally activate the insurance coverage. Because the insurance companies don't want the cases to go to trial where the laws could be exposed to change, they usually offer a reasonable settlement before trial. Even though acceptance of a settlement offer does not help future wrongful death cases, it is difficult for me to advise a client not to accept the money. To go to a trial solely to be the test case for future malpractice claims is not a solution for the distressed pet owner.

Two months later I took my dogs to Aspen for the weekend. While I was playing golf with my brother, I didn't want to leave my dogs alone all day, so I set up an arrangement with the local veterinary hospital to day board them. They even gave me a key so I could drop the dogs off and pick them up. The dogs were out of the heat, and they enjoyed being with the other dogs. One afternoon when I was coming back to pick them up I met Samantha Monahan, a wholesome looking red-haired twentyish woman who was sitting outdoors next to a beautiful Bernese mountain dog.

"That's a beautiful dog," I complimented her.

"Thanks," she replied. "But Brandy has a broken back."

"A broken back?" I questioned, horrified. "How did that happen?"

"A cab driver hit him," she replied.

"Intentionally?"

"Yes," she replied to my shock and disgust. I could feel the hair on my head stand up as I thought of this beautiful animal being mowed down by a car.

"Tell me what happened," I pleaded.

"He got out one night. I went looking for him but I never found him. Then Tim Morrison, a veterinarian, called me. Brandy had been dropped off there by the police. Apparently an independent cab driver in town had picked up a drunk passenger, but the driver was drunk himself. According to the passenger, the driver had said, 'Hey, watch this' as he mowed Brandy down. According to the police report, Brandy flew fifty feet in the air. His back was broken and now he's paralyzed."

I shuddered just hearing the story. I had to do something. I sat down next to her and told her, "I'm a dog lawyer." She looked up with interest.

"I have an attorney here in town, but he doesn't seem to be getting anywhere with the case," Sam replied sadly.

"Have him call me," I told her as I handed her my card. "I'll consult with him for no charge."

I picked up my dogs and headed back to Denver still thinking about the maliciousness of someone injuring Sam's dog.

The next week I received a call from Sam's attorney, Todd Rogers, who was representing her in her suit against the cab driver. "I've been frustrated," he said, "when I discovered there's no law in Colorado permitting the recovery of punitive damages for the intentional killing of a pet."

Punitive damages allow a person to recover money from someone who did something to them that deserves to be punished even though there may not be very large economic damages otherwise. In California, a dog owner is entitled to recover punitive damages for the intentional killing of a pet. New York also allows punitive damages, but many other states do not.

Rogers went on, "I was going to wait to see what the criminal courts will rule in a case against the cab driver for cruelty to animals."

It was possible that the criminal court judge would allow Sam to recover damages, which at this point had exceeded $10,000 in veterinarian costs. Of course, this was not a wrongful death case, but the dog, still alive, had been gravely injured. The veterinarian had him in rehabilitation. But it had been the veterinarians at Hartsdale University where they had performed the state-of-the-art surgeries to preserve his life who had invested thousands of dollars in medical treatment, not to mention the airfare from Aspen. This had cost Sam more than she could ever repay in an effort to preserve the life of Brandy, her beloved pet.

Sam was working part-time at the medical clinic to repay her debt to the veterinarians there. She still owed a substantial sum to Hartsdale.

Sam was hoping that the cab driver would be ordered to pay her the medical bills at his criminal trial. But since the cab driver worked for an independent cab company, there was no one who had the money to pay the medical bills. In this case, even if he had worked for a major cab company, his behavior had probably been intentional and therefore outside the scope of any employment, relieving any employer from financial liability for his actions. Sam's only hope was in the criminal courts.

Because cruelty to animals is a misdemeanor, the fine imposed would not exceed five hundred dollars. It is unusual to order a defendant to pay restitution in excess of a fine and in excess of what the victim would recover from the defendant in civil court. The judge found the driver guilty of cruelty to animals, but ordered no restitution and no jail time. Sam was stuck with all of the medical expenses of trying to preserve her dog's life. Two months later I heard that Brandy had died.

In many cases I have handled, dogs are killed while traveling on airplanes. Unfortunately, the pilot and employees of the airlines generally know, or should know, that the pets traveling below are going to die because of heat and suffocation when there is a delay on a hot runway, but they make an economic decision. It could cost thousands of dollars for an airline to have its aircraft return to the gate to get a dog a drink of water. Instead the planes sit on the tarmac waiting to take off. Officials know the dog will die, and yet employees tell the passenger the dog will be fine. They know that if the dog dies the airline will only be liable for the insured luggage value, rather than penalized a much larger amount by the FAA for delayed travel.

Pierce Roland and his wife, Julie, were flying from Seattle to Austin, via Dallas. They requested information about the heat in Dallas numerous times while waiting at the gate in Seattle. They often flew with their yellow Labrador retriever, Banner.

"How is the temperature in Dallas?" Pierce asked the clerk. "We have our dog with us and we won't fly him if it is too hot." Being familiar with the hazards of flying an animal in high temperatures, the Rolands had brought Julie's father who lived in Seattle to the airport with them. If it were too hot to fly Banner, they would leave him with Julie's father.

"It's not too hot," the attendant at the check-in counter told Pierce. "Your dog will be fine." Banner was put in his airline crate and checked onto the flight. The flight was delayed thirty minutes. While waiting at the gate, Pierce repeatedly told the gate attendant, "My dog is on this flight. If it is too hot for him we will retrieve him from the plane."

"It's perfectly safe for your dog. Don't worry," Pierce was told at the gate.

Once on the plane everything proceeded normally until Pierce and Julie arrived in Dallas. They were told that their flight to Austin was delayed for a half hour. Pierce once again spoke to the gate attendant, "Our dog is on this flight. Can we check on him?"

"Your dog is fine," Pierce was told. "They would tell us if anything were wrong with him."

Pierce waited, not too convinced that everything was okay with Banner. Once Julie and Pierce boarded the plane Pierce again told the flight attendant that he was concerned about Banner because of the heat and the delays.

"Your dog is fine. You will have to take your seat," he was told. When the plane was delayed another half hour after everyone had boarded the aircraft, Pierce got out of his seat to ask to check on Banner and was ordered by the flight attendant to remain seated. While seated, Pierce and Julie saw a large dog kennel being loaded onto the plane sideways. Becoming very alarmed, Pierce again contacted the flight attendant only to be told that Banner was fine and he would need to remain seated and stop worrying.

Upon arrival in Austin, Julie and Pierce rushed to the baggage claim to rescue Banner. After a seemingly endless wait, a baggage handler called out, "Mr. Roland?"

"That's me," an anxious Pierce responded.

"We're sorry," the handler said. "But your dog didn't make it."

At first Pierce thought the handler meant that Banner had not made the flight to Austin. He hesitated as the handler continued, "What do you want us to do with him?"

"You mean he's dead?" Julie cried out.

"I'm afraid so, Ma'am," the handler replied, anxious to get back to less emotional work. "We have his crate here. You may want to file a claim in the Baggage Claim Office."

Pierce and Julie were in shock. Banner was dead and they didn't know what to do. At the claim office they filled out all of the "lost luggage" claim forms and returned to their home without Banner. They had requested that the dog's body be sent to their veterinarian for an autopsy. It was determined that he had died from heat prostration. A few weeks later the Rolands received a letter from the airline that stated, "We are sorry about your lost 'luggage.' Please accept one thousand dollars as insured by your ticket." They then called me wanting to sue the airlines for wrongful death of their dog. But because of the liability waiver the airlines place on each ticket, I was unable to proceed against the airlines with any chance for success.

Beating the airline's contract with the passenger to only insure the "luggage" for $1000 has been difficult. Owners have been forced to sit on the aircraft while they listened to their dog howl to death, only to learn that the airline treats their dog as luggage after death as much as it did prior to death. As appalling as it may seem, dogs on airlines are treated as cargo. Twenty-four puppies died of heat prostration when a flight from Chicago to San Diego was delayed on a hot day at Chicago's O'Hare Airport. The sellers had been a puppy mill in the Midwest which was shipping the puppies to pet stores in Southern California. Neither party to the contracts was concerned about the puppies because they had been insured. They were simply treated as perishable goods that had perished in flight, just as if they had been crates of oranges.

Sometimes, taking a case into their own hands is the only recourse for the pet owner. It was not until a cat was lost on an airline out of New York and was thought to be alive in the aircraft traveling all over the world that there was enough public outcry to cause the aircraft to be grounded and searched until the cat could be found. In Los Angeles, a family had lost their pet poodle during travel from LAX. The dog was spotted running loose on the property of LAX. Because all of the property is fenced in, the dog could not be recovered. Airport officials refused to allow the owners on the property and refused to stop flights to permit the dog to be retrieved. The owners took the case to the media. Neighbors around the airport agreed to watch for the dog. When they found the dog near the fence, they called the owner who dug a hole under the fence, crawled under, and retrieved his dog.

I was still looking for the case that would change the treatment of wrongful death by the courts. I thought I might have it in the Martinez problem. The case began auspiciously.

"Come get your dog. He's vomiting all over the place!" the groomer shouted to eighteen-year-old Shelly Martinez, a clerk at an ABC pet superstore.

"Don't forget to punch out," the manager called as Shelly left her post to run to the rescue of her dog who had been left at the grooming department that morning.

Shelly had thought her new job at the pet superstore would be a good opportunity to get some fringe benefits, such as the grooming of her family's dogs at a discount. For her father's birthday she wanted to surprise him by taking his show quality red chow, Rusty, to be groomed. She had arranged with her mother that morning to take the dog with her without her father noticing and return the dog fully groomed for the dinner birthday party that night.

In addition, Shelly had arranged with the head of the grooming department to bring the dog in at 9:00 a.m. and be ready to go at 5:00 p.m. She dropped the dog off on schedule.

At lunch break Shelly went to check on her dog. He hadn't been groomed yet, so she took him with her to lunch in the side yard. She gave him water and returned him at 1:00 p.m. to the grooming department.

Now, tearful and upset at what the groomer had told her, Shelly found Rusty. No one offered any help. The petite young woman pulled the dazed, seventy-pound dog, who must have stayed without water or fresh air for four hours when he went into convulsions and began vomiting, out to her car. She hoisted him into the vehicle by herself and then raced across town to the only veterinarian she knew. After being worked on for nearly two hours, Rusty died. The cause of death was heat prostration. Shelly had to return home to her father's happy birthday party with sad news. His prized and much loved dog had died.

Shelly tried to get the store to take responsibility. They referred her to the insurance company. After the insurance company denied any liability and after Shelly had been fired for no apparent reason, the family came to me. "What can you do to force the store to take responsibility for causing our dog's death and causing our family so much grief?" Mr. Martinez asked.

Establishing damages in a wrongful death case is the most difficult aspect. Although some states allow emotional distress damages, most states like Colorado, where this incident took place, do not. Therefore, it is necessary to establish the highest economic value for the dog in order to receive any compensation for the owners for the suffering they have sustained. I also felt the store should pay for intentional infliction of emotional distress for the outrageous way the store employees had treated Shelly.

I was able to establish that Rusty had had a unique value as a stud dog, because he was a red chow that had the genes to produce rare blue chows. Thus, the economic value of the dog or its replacement value could be established at about $15,000. I would need more ammunition, however, to get a higher recovery. Because I believed the store's behavior and treatment of my client to be outrageous, I called the local television station. Like me, they were outraged. They went to the store to try to get a statement from them. When asked about the case, an employee stated, "Those owners knew that dog was sick when they brought it in here. It's their fault he died."

Now I not only had a case for wrongful death of the dog, but I was able to add a claim for defamation of my clients. Their dog had not been sick. The employee had confused the Martinezes' dog with another dog that had also died at that grooming department. In order to avoid much more complicated and notorious litigation, the store's insurance company agreed to settle for damages of $24,000. Although this was the largest award for the wrongful death of a dog, it was partially due to the store's own fault in making a defamatory statement on television. But, to my surprise, the fact that defamation had resulted in the large settlement caused an unfortunate outcome. The press picked up coverage of the case as being "the largest settlement ever" for the wrongful death of a dog. The television show American Journal interviewed the Martinez family and included a segment on wrongful death of dogs in their program. Soon many people across the country called me, wanting to sue for the wrongful deaths of their dogs. But I knew it was not likely they would ever get the recovery the Martinez family had received. With my desire to help wronged animals, it was difficult to turn their hopefulness down.

Although the Martinez case gave me a rare opportunity to right a wrong, I have handled many cases for wrongful death over the years, and none has been strong enough to change the law in its jurisdiction. Most of the cases settle for a reasonable amount in damages before the case can be tried on appeal. Even though it seems unfair, the majority of victims of a wrongful death of a dog claim are unable to recover anything.

11

No Cash Refunds

June Patterson was on welfare and had an adolescent son, Joey, who had Down's syndrome. She barely had enough money to support herself and Joey. But June had been depressed, so one afternoon she and Joey went for a walk in one of the Denver shopping malls. When they entered the mall pet store, they were greeted by white, brown, and black puppies with sad eyes and wagging tails.

"Come see our puppies," a clerk hailed June and Joey when he saw them.

June looked around to see Joey stooped down near the pen smiling.

The clerk watched her. "Is there one dog in particular you would like to see?"

"Oh yes," June replied. "That little Yorkshire terrier is so darling."

The clerk reached into the pen and pulled out the

Yorkshire terrier puppy. He weighed no more than two pounds.

"He looks so happy with you," the clerk told June as she cuddled the puppy in her arms. Joey was stroking the puppy's head as the clerk continued with his hard sell tactics. "A puppy is a real comfort, you know."

"He's so darling!" June exclaimed. "How much is he?"

"He's a special puppy," the clerk answered, dodging the question. "He comes from a long line of purebreds. He has a pedigree that would permit you to breed him and sell the puppies for as much as you pay for him. You should be able to get a stud fee for him of nearly a thousand dollars."

The strategy for selling these puppies had been perfected. The clerks knew all the right things to say. They told June all the right things about how right the puppy was for her and how, if she didn't buy it, it might never get a good home and on and on and on. What they said was just what the lonely, depressed and broke woman sought to hear. If she bought this puppy, she would be happy. June agreed to purchase the puppy for $750. She carried the puppy in her arms to the checkout counter as Joey, still smiling, followed behind.

"Here is our sales contract," the cashier told June as she passed the contract across the counter. "Everyone who buys a puppy has to sign this."

"I don't have my glasses with me," June told the girl.

"It's just a sales agreement," the clerk said, without explaining any of the guarantees or any disclaimers. The sales contract was one legal page of single space type. I later came to suspect that June could barely read, with or without her glasses, and even if she could have read the contract, she would never have understood the legal language. June gave the clerk her check, signed on the dotted line, and owned the puppy.

"When you get your puppy home," the sales clerk said, "you should feed him cottage cheese and rice."

Not understanding that such a menu was unusual, June did not question the clerk. She did not know that this formula is often fed to dogs with diarrhea, a symptom of distemper.

June took the puppy she named Tyke home after purchasing collars and bed and blankets and toys for her new "baby." But when she got Tyke home, he began to vomit. June wrapped him in blankets and took him into her bed with her. Soon, though, Tyke began convulsing and urinating on the bed. June called the office of an emergency veterinarian.

"My puppy is really sick. He's vomiting and shaking and I don't know what to do."

"Bring him in here right away," the receptionist at the twenty-four-hour hospital told her.

June immediately rushed the dog there, where it was placed on intravenous feeding. Tyke was treated for thirty-six hours at the veterinary clinic. He appeared to have recovered and was released to June who now had a $450 veterinary bill. June took the puppy home and cared for him as recommended. That evening he went into convulsions again and died in June's arms.

Now June had lost the puppy, which had symbolized happiness to her, she had suffered three unbearably stressful and grief-ridden days, and she was out $750 and owed an additional $450. She called the pet store.

"I purchased a puppy at your store last Saturday and he died," June sobbed to the clerk. "What should I do?"

"Read your contract," the clerk told her. "It says no guarantees and, anyway, no cash refunds. Oh, and we only pay vet bills if you take the dog to one of our veterinarians. Since you didn't call us first, no vet bills will be paid."

June was grief-stricken, then horrified, then angry. When she told her only friend about all that had happened to her, the friend suggested June call me. June called me the next morning.

After June described to me all that she had been through, I reviewed the pet store's contract. It stated NO CASH REFUNDS and, based on that statement, the store was refusing to give June her money back. Despite the appearance that the contract would be binding and June would have no recourse, I told her, "There are two provisions of law that allow the buyer recourse regardless of what the contract says."

The implied warranty of merchantability is implied in all contracts for the sale of goods. It states that it is implied that goods being sold are merchantable, and the only way such a warranty can be avoided is by clear and predominant language disclaiming the warranty. Certainly a dog is not considered merchantable if it is deathly ill at the time of sale.

Another provision of the law that benefits the buyer is the law of unconscionability. A contract cannot be interpreted so as to result in an unconscionable result for the buyer. A contract which requires a buyer that has no pets to purchase $750 in pet supplies is unconscionable. A contract that requires a buyer who purchased a Yorkshire terrier to take a poodle or other breed of dog in replacement or otherwise lose their money is unconscionable. Dogs are not fungible goods. Replacing one dog with another if the buyer does not want any other dog is unconscionable as is forcing a person to become a pet owner.

Based upon these provisions of law, I called Bob Martin, the pet store owner. "June should at least get her money back," I told him.

Martin, the owner of many stores, would not even discuss settlement. He said, "If you want to sue us, go ahead. We always win."

I was furious at his heartless attitude. "We will recover against your store for the veterinary expenses and emotional distress damages for the loss of the pet," I told him. The law in Colorado did not allow for emotional distress damages for the owner of a dog that dies, but case law in other jurisdictions did allow such recoveries and I felt we could pose the argument and let the judge decide what remedy June deserved.

So I sued him. The case was ordered to be decided before a magistrate in the Denver District Court. Henry William, the white-haired magistrate, sat at the head of a long conference table. Slick-haired Bob Martin and three sales clerks sat on one side of the table without an attorney. June and I sat on the other side.

The magistrate reviewed the complaint and answer while we all sat in silence. When he questioned June about the instruction to feed the puppy rice and cottage cheese, Martin very cockily interrupted the magistrate to tell him, "We can't be responsible for all of the puppies that get sold through my store." The magistrate quickly interrupted Martin and put him in his place.

"Don't speak until you are spoken to in my courtroom."

Martin paid no attention and began to argue his case. The magistrate slammed down his gavel. "Don't come in here again," he told Martin, "without an attorney to represent you."

The magistrate willingly accepted all of the case law I had prepared from over a dozen jurisdictions outside of Colorado, even in Canada, and said he would take the case under consideration.

Suddenly Martin saw that this magistrate was not on his side and would not support his position that it was legal to rip off poor distressed women with no money.

The next day Martin had an attorney call me. "My client has offered to compensate your client for her veterinary bills, refund her money, and pay a token payment for emotional distress," he conveyed. Because June and Joey so desperately needed the money, we accepted the settlement.

The next day an article was printed in the Denver Post recounting the case without the confidential results of the settlement. As a result, I received seventeen calls from other buyers of pets from the same store who had the same thing happen to them. The store has since rewritten its contract and changed its policy regarding cash refunds.

Purchasing a dog from a pet store is not the only place a buyer must beware of the contract. Breeders also generally sell dogs with contracts. The contract can be one for a pet quality puppy or a show quality puppy. Usually, show quality puppies involve more warranties than the pet qualities. In either case, the buyer must carefully review what is being warranted by the seller.

Often, genetic health defects that are typical of the breed are warranted. The issue is usually how long the warranty is for, and what needs to be done to activate the warranty.

For example, in the contract I received when I purchased Dar, the breeder warranted against hip dysplasia for two years. The contract required that the dog be x-rayed at one year, and, if diagnosed with dysplasia, x-rayed by the breeder's veterinarian. If the diagnosis was confirmed, a replacement dog would be given. The breeder's veterinarian confirmed the diagnosis.

However, usually hip dysplasia cannot be diagnosed at one year. The OFA does not accept x-rays taken before the dog is two years old. Unfortunately for this breeder, the entire litter of nine puppies had hip dysplasia.

Feeling sorry for the breeder, who I do not think knew that her dog or the sire could produce dysplastic dogs, I called her.

"Please," she said, "come look at an adult dog I recently imported from Germany for breeding purposes." The dog, I was told, was a seven-year-old female Schutzhund III that had not taken during her last breeding.

"I don't need another dog yet, and certainly not a seven-year-old dog," I kept insisting. But once I met Anke I knew she would come home with us.

Not all breeders are willing to comply with their own guarantees. They put them into the contract knowing that the buyers expect them, but when the time comes to pay off they will request that the original dog be returned to them to be put to sleep before they permit the buyer to take a "replacement" dog. The breeder knows that the buyer is by this time too attached to the dog to allow it to be put to sleep solely because of a health defect, and so the buyer, scared off, never claims on the warranty. Once again the law of unconscionability will apply. It would be an unconscionable result to have a healthy dog put to sleep in order to activate a warranty. These situations can usually be overcome. Only if the breeder can show that that dog being alive will injure his or her reputation will the damages be there to warrant putting the dog to sleep. But if the owner has no intention of showing the dog, then breeder reputation is not at issue, and there is no excuse to have the dog terminated.

Many states have enacted lemon laws which permit the buyer to recover against the breeder for the veterinary expenses, and/or receive a replacement dog. Although these laws can be harsh for breeders, they generally only apply to breeders who breed quite a few dogs per year. The intent is to force breeders to investigate their lines carefully before selling a dog with a genetic defect. In some cases, the breeder really doesn't know that a specific breeding will result in a genetic defect. Nonetheless, under the lemon laws, they are liable for any resulting damages.

The requirement that the breeder compensate the owner for the veterinary expenses is the most important aspect of the lemon laws, because, often, as with Dar, the expense of "repairing" the dog's defect is much greater than the purchase price of the dog. When Dar's hips degenerated to the point they were affecting his lifestyle, my husband, Jerry, and I had an orthopedic surgeon perform a hip replacement on him. Only those who love a dog can understand the depths of an owner's love and loyalty.

In one dispute I handled pursuant to a coownership agreement, the buyer, Joanna Edwards, agreed to purchase a terrier with a herniated umbilical. The dog was purchased for $400 pursuant to a coownership agreement in which Joanna agreed to allow the seller, Alice Solby, to show the dog.

When Joanna took the puppy to her veterinarian to fix the herniated umbilical, the vet refused to do the surgery without spaying the dog at the same time. "The American Veterinary Medical Associations's Ethics Code requires that a veterinarian not perform a surgery on a dog that may be bred or shown which will cover up the genetic defect. It is required that the dog be spayed or neutered at the same time," he explained.

Joanna got three additional opinions supporting this position. Solby refused to comply. She wanted to keep the dog intact so the dog could be shown. Solby got an injunction preventing the dog from being spayed. The veterinarians refused to perform corrective surgery on the dog without simultaneously performing the spay surgery. Joanna feared for her dog's life and didn't want to do anything that might jeopardize her.

After I went through lengthy negotiations and many court filings and the passing of the dog's eight-month birthday, the case settled. My client was permitted to keep the dog and perform the surgeries by paying a fee to compensate the seller for the loss of a show prospect.

Once again, the lengths to which a dog lover would go to ensure the health and well-being of a pet went well beyond love, and the pet's purchase price.

12

Who Gets Custody of Bowser?

One warm, full-mooned summer night in San Diego, I took Dar to an area called "Dog Beach" where dogs could be off leash at all times. The dogs socialize and it's not too bad a spot for their owners as well.

Dar and I strolled along the silver, moon-washed sand for a few minutes. Then I stopped to look out at the dark velvety sea. A man with a collie walked up beside me. "Beautiful, isn't it?" he said. We started talking and he told me how he had been traveling across the country with his dog, Sam.

"Dogs are great traveling companions and good friends in general," I said.

He gave a half smile and said, "Yeah, I know what you mean. The women come and go, but the dog remains the same."

I have often thought of his comments as I deal with separating and divorcing couples involved in disputes over their pets. After I had handled quite a few custody disputes both in California and Colorado, my reputation became known and I was interviewed by the New York Times about people and their pets during divorce. One of the first questions the reporter asked was, "Why do you think custody disputes over pets are so common these days?"

"Because the world is so transient," I replied. "Husbands and wives come and go, kids move away from home, jobs change quickly. People have come to fear change in their lives because they can't control it. But, when it comes to pets, suddenly they have something they can love and become attached to, without fear that they will ever lose it. The dog won't walk out on them. They feel like they have bonded for life."

"But why the custody disputes?" the reporter continued.

"Because the dog is a symbol to both people of their love and lovability, if they keep the dog, they have someone to love and someone to love them. It is the only source of stability in their lives," I answered, and I still believe that today. I also think that is why dog law has become so important to so many people. There is finally a legal way to protect the relationship between an owner and his beloved pet.

However, dog custody disputes are the nastiest of dog law cases. Generally, divorce law does not provide for the major cause of the contest between spouses: who gets the pets? Pets are treated as property and their division is treated according to state law in the same manner as the division of a dining room table. But, as pet owners know, this doesn't always work. In court decisions, custody is not based upon the best interest of the dog, as it is with children, but upon the greatest right of ownership since the animal is construed to be "property." Therefore, even if one spouse is moving to a home with a yard where the dog can run while the other is moving into a one-bedroom apartment where the dog will be confined all day, the apartment dweller may get the dog.

In the California case of Benton vs. Benton, the assets of the short-lived marriage were a $250,000 home, its furnishings, and an sheepdog named Snickers. Tom Benton, a balding mid-thirtyish owner of a television sales and repair shop, elected to keep the house and furniture. His petite wife, Barbara, once a cheerleader, left and took Snickers with her. When Tom learned that three-year-old Snickers was living in an apartment with Barbara, he fought for custody of the dog. Since the divorce decree had become final, he had to bargain with Barbara. Tom offered Barbara the house and furniture, so long as Snickers would be turned over to him. Barbara refused. Tom then requested to at least have visitation with Snickers, and Barbara agreed. She brought Snickers to spend the day at Tom's house, which was next door to his store, while she went to work. When she objected because Tom didn't stay home to dog-sit, Tom panicked and moved Snickers to a friend's house in Nevada, hoping to avoid the California divorce court's jurisdiction. Then Tom called me, hoping I could help him get full custody of Snickers.

"I have to have him," Tom insisted. "I can't bear to have him locked up in an apartment all day."

"Did the divorce decree specify where Barbara had to live with the dog?" I questioned, sure that it did not since dogs were considered property.

"No," he answered. "But he can't live in an apartment."

"But your taking him was stealing her property," I informed him, attempting to explain that he had no legal grounds to take the dog. "Why don't you return the dog to Barbara and set up a visitation agreement with her so you can keep the dog at your house some of the time?" I suggested.

"I'll give her the house," he persisted, "and all of the furnishings, so long as I can have Snickers."

"Why didn't you suggest that at the divorce settlement?" I questioned him.

"I didn't know how much I would miss him," Tom replied. "Please take the case." He pleaded with me to help him right the wrong.

"I can't," I told him. "The divorce decree is final. But I will help you negotiate a visitation agreement with your ex-wife."

"Okay." He sighed heavily. "I'll call you back if I decide to do that."

A few days later he called again and I arranged a visitation agreement which placated but really didn't satisfy him.

Because visitation agreements assume the most cooperative of solutions, they don't always work out that well when a couple is in the throes of divorce and separation. In their separation agreement, Billy and Rachel agreed to joint custody of their yellow Labrador, Bouncer, out of concern for "the best interest of the dog." Billy and Rachel had lived together for nearly five years and had purchased Bouncer during that time. Because they had not been married, the couple was not faced with a judge's order, but could determine their own resolution. They agreed that Rachel would keep Bouncer overnight for protection and company. Each morning after Rachel left for work, Billy would come by the house and take Bouncer jogging with him and keep the dog throughout the day if he chose, so long as Bouncer was back at Rachel's house by the time she returned from work. Rachel and Billy alternated custody of Bouncer on weekends. Things worked out amicably until Rachel got a new boyfriend. While coming to pick up Bouncer on weekends, Billy would linger to check out the new guy. To spite Rachel, he did not return Bouncer on time. Rachel got very upset.

I received a call from Billy who asked me to arrange a joint custody agreement for the two of them. While we were still negotiating the terms of the agreement, more conflict arose. Rachel came over to Billy's house to retrieve Bouncer. Billy refused to let her in. He then called me, screaming, "Rachel's here and she wants Bouncer. What should I do?"

"Billy, is it her turn to have him?" I asked, trying to calm him down.

"Yes, but I don't want . . . She's breaking the window!" he screamed into the phone. "Call nine-one-one! Call nine-one-one! I gotta go." The line went dead. I called 911 and gave them Billy's address telling them it was a domestic dispute. I did not tell them it was over a dog for fear they might not show up. The police arrived to find a broken window and a missing dog. Rachel had disappeared with Bouncer. Billy never saw them again.

Without written agreements, joint custody of a beloved animal can be difficult to control. Ben and Mary Jordan, who had decided to end their nine-year union, arranged every detail for their joint custody agreement which I had been hired to prepare for Ben. It was agreed that their white terrier, Mitzy, would be picked up for weekend visits on Friday evenings at a friend's house and returned by five on Sundays. The exchange would not only take place each weekend, but every holiday as well.

For several weeks everything worked well, and then the first holiday came along. Both Ben and Mary wanted to be with Mitzy. They agreed to spend Thanksgiving together "for Mitzy's sake." A few days later a sheepish Ben called. "We've decided to get back together and this time we're going to stay together to be a family for Mitzy's sake."

In preparing a visitation agreement for a couple who, though they will separate, will share a child or pet, it is important to spell out every detail of the new relationship. For example, who will provide for medical treatment if the animal is injured? What if one says do the surgery and the other says no? Or if one can't afford it? Or, if the injury to the dog was caused by the negligence of one of the owners, who pays the bill? What if one owner moves out of state, remarries, buys new pets?

Though a written agreement spells out terms more clearly, evidence of an agreement can also be established by a pattern of behavior. When Janice and Brian Frank came to see me seeking custody of a nine-year-old Newfoundland named Warren, they explained that Brian's ex-girlfriend Samantha had sued the Franks for replevin to get custody of Warren. Brian had lived with Samantha until Warren was three years old. There was never any question that Warren had originally been purchased by Brian. Brian paid all the expenses for Warren and had been the primary caregiver for the dog. But, when the couple split up, Brian took a job out of state where he could not take Warren with him. Samantha agreed to keep Warren along with her own dog, Molly. It was agreed that Brian would pay all medical expenses for Warren as well as all food and incidental expense. Brian regularly sent checks to the local veterinarian where Warren received his care and grooming and special dog food. When Brian returned from Alaska a year and a half later, he had married Janice and tried to reclaim Warren. However, Samantha couldn't bear to give him up. For some time the Franks and Samantha and her new husband, Richard Drake, tried joint custody of Warren. But Samantha often refused to return Warren as agreed and the Franks finally refused to share Warren. The relationship between the two couples rapidly deteriorated, and the Drakes sued the Franks for replevin. Although the suit seemed a frivolous one, Samantha's husband was an attorney and she begged him to do something, so he filed the suit.

At the hearing to determine custody pending trial, I argued, "Brian has paid all of the expenses for Warren, and Samantha has paid all of the expenses for Molly. Therefore," I said, "Brian has never relinquished ownership rights to Warren even though Samantha had custody of Warren for over one year."

The judge agreed and granted the Franks custody of Warren pending trial. The Drakes must have found better things to do, because they never proceeded with the case. A year later it was dismissed and Warren stayed with Brian, his rightful owner.

Even when they are specifically drafted, joint custody agreements can be troublesome. Sarah and Mike Hayes, a red-haired couple who looked enough alike to be twins, squabbled throughout their eight-year marriage and their divorce. It shouldn't have been a surprise when she sued him for three years of back dog support of their two dogs as soon as he announced he was remarrying. Joint custody of the dogs had been agreed to in the divorce papers of Hayes vs. Hayes. The couple also agreed to pay expenses of the dogs, a yellow Lab named Trevor and a husky mix named Sheba, equally and to share equal time with the dogs. However, a few months later, my client, Sarah, who had primary custody, purchased another dog. The new dog, a shepherd mix named Samson, hated Mike Hayes at first sight. Whenever Mike came to visit Trevor and Sheba, the new dog attacked him. Finally, Mike gave up. For over three years he did not see Trevor. During this time, Sarah didn't ask Mike to support the dogs. Then Mike decided to remarry. When Sarah learned of the pending event, she sued Mike for three years of back dog support. Mike claimed he had been prevented from visitation, violating the agreement, and therefore he was not liable for expenses of maintenance of the dogs.

Sarah claimed Mike owed half of everything she'd paid out during the three-year period. She laboriously itemized the purchases, from flea dip, grooming, carpet cleaning, dog food, new leashes and equipment, to the tune of $10,000. Fortunately, I was able to get Mike to agree to a reasonable amount, and Sarah was granted sole custody. If custody or visitation is to be agreed upon, every specific foreseeable event must be discussed in the agreement or there will be a dispute and, in this case, though Sarah was my client, I'd learned to know her well enough to judge such a detailed agreement was an absolute necessity.

Though dog custody disputes are tricky even if the animals remain healthy and happy, the most difficult disputes come when one party decides to put the dogs to sleep, because of an injury or old age, and the co-owners do not agree. What should they do? In all of my agreements, I put in a clause that allows the person who agrees to pay for medical treatment, even though considered excessive by the other person, to then acquire full ownership of the dog.

In a New York case, I was called by a distressed ex-husband. Malcolm Sewell's ex-wife, Marcia, had his beloved Airedale put to sleep at the time of their divorce. The divorce judge ruled that the action was solely done to punish Malcolm. New York allows for punitive damages for the intentional killing of a pet.

Malcolm wanted to file suit for the intentional destruction of joint property. Criminal cruelty laws may also have applied. I was willing to assist Malcolm as co-counsel but no New York attorney would take the case. There was just not enough money in the intentional killing of dog cases. Without New York counsel, even though Marcia was obviously liable, there was not much he could do. Even with punitive damages, the fair market value of the dog would be little more than five hundred dollars.

Despite the outrageous conduct of the wife in intentionally killing her ex-husband's dog, there was little that could be done against the wife since legally the dog was marriage property and she had as much right to control its destiny as he did, so long as she compensated him for half of the dog's value. But, as every dog owner knows, it is not the value of the dog the owner wants to recover, it is the dog.

One breezy summer day a pretty young woman with waist-length blond hair dressed in the latest grunge attire entered my office.

"Hello, I'm Beth Wright," she explained. "I own twelve purebred Belgian sheepdogs which I breed as a hobby and for profit."

"Sit down and make yourself comfortable," I said. "Then you can tell me all about it."

She settled herself on my couch, drawing her knees up and clasping them with her arms. Then she began to speak in a tearful voice. "When I got divorced, my husband, Richard, was granted ownership of six of the dogs since they were considered assets of the marriage."

I nodded. "Go on."

"Well, Richard, acting like the jerk he is, then placed the dogs in animal shelters because he had only taken them to spite me. I didn't know that Richard had abandoned my dogs until I received a call from the animal control saying a group of Belgian sheepdogs had been impounded. When I went to the pound, I discovered that the dogs were mine."

The trouble came when the Boulder Animal Control would not release the dogs to Beth unless the animals were spayed and neutered first. Although the shelter's policy was certainly noble and worthwhile in light of the number of dogs put to sleep each year, it was only salt in the wound to Beth. If she did not agree to neuter and spay the dogs, they would be destroyed. If she agreed, she would have to maintain and own six dogs that were perfect specimens of their breed, show and breeding dogs which would never be able to be shown again. "Richard has found the perfect revenge," she said. Tears ran down her cheeks.

I calmed her down and called the kennel on Beth's behalf. Then I negotiated a settlement in which it was agreed that Beth would grant a large amount of money for the spaying and neutering of future animals in the kennel so long as her show animals were released intact.

When you're involved in the novel specialty of dog law, you must be ready to use your ingenuity and wits to find a solution even when there is no precedent in the law to guide you. After all, navigating uncharted waters is the name of the game.

When Amy Lippman, who was involved in a divorce action in Colorado, told me she was afraid that her husband,

Paul, would get the dog, Sandy, a Yorkshire terrier, in their divorce action and that her husband was the most unreasonable man in the world, I applied my best Solomon attitude. Despite a court order instructing each of them not to dispose of marital property, Amy told me, "I sold Sandy to my cousin, Bill Thomas. When Paul learned of the transfer, he demanded that Sandy be returned to the home. I felt remorseful for my actions and agreed." She called Bill and told him that she had to get Sandy back because she had been wrong in trying to hide him from Paul. Although it had not even been a week since the transfer, Bill's wife, Jean, refused to return the dog. Now neither Amy nor Paul had their dog, and Amy was in violation of a court order. Bill and Jean then claimed that they had purchased Sandy in good faith and refused to return the dog.

"What a mess," Amy said dejectedly.

I had to agree.

Under the law, Amy owed Paul one half of Sandy's value and would face the consequences of disposing of marital property, but both Amy and Paul wanted Sandy back. After a lengthy and expensive dispute with the Thomases, who were unable to prove that they had ever actually purchased Sandy and could not disprove Amy's contention that she had merely asked them to care for Sandy until the divorce was over, Bill and Jean agreed to return Sandy to Amy and Paul. Then we met to try to resolve the remaining problem of how Amy and Paul could share their dog though they no longer shared a life.

Under most state laws, dogs and other pets are deemed personal property, and their division is treated like any other personal property. The spouse with greater ownership rights may be more persuasive in getting custody of the dog although he or she may have to compensate the other spouse with property of equal value. If one spouse can show that the dog was hers before the marriage and was cared for from her separate property, not marital money, or purchased with separate money even if during the marriage, then she should have no problem in winning custody of the dog. In a community property state, if the dog was purchased during the marriage regardless of who paid for the dog, it is owned equally by both parties and must be shared equally, or again, offset by property of equal value.

The law is so harsh on pets in a divorce case because they are treated as property. The best protection for couples is to provide for the pets upon marriage in a prenuptial agreement, or during divorce in a separation agreement. The courts will generally recognize any agreements between the parties, and it is most likely that the owners can determine what is best for their pet better than the judge will in divorce court.

It is not only separating couples who fight over custody of a dog. Often, breeders retain an ownership interest in a dog that they sell. Breeders want to have the right to breed a dog if it turns out to be a good show prospect. They also want to be able to control whether or not the dog is shown. A good show dog can be very valuable to a breeding kennel. Because breeders can't keep all of the puppies, they often sell the puppies pursuant to a co-ownership agreement, so they can have some rights to the dog but not have to raise and socialize the dog from puppyhood. Unfortunately for everyone, co-ownership agreements often lead to disputes.

The buyer in a co-ownership agreement dispute is usually a neophyte to dog showing or breeding. This was especially true in the case I handled for Brenda Harrison who had purchased her first standard poodle with full intention of showing the dog. Dark haired, vivacious, and only twenty-one, Brenda was a groomer by trade and wanted to become a handler of show poodles. She purchased a puppy, whom she called Elliot after an old boyfriend, from Rita Lorree, a woman she believed to be a reputable breeder who sold the dog pursuant to a co-ownership contract. The pertinent provisions of the contract required that the dog be shown "to a championship." It also required that the dog not begin showing until he was two years old.

When Brenda first came into my office, she was accompanied by her parents. After they had checked in at the reception desk, I took them all to my office.

"I understand that you have lost a dog?" I began.

Brenda's face reddened. "He was stolen."

Her mother chimed in, "They took him."

Then her father took up the cause. "Can you get him back?"

"We want him," Brenda cried.

"We do," said her mother, "very definitely."

Her father spoke up simultaneously, and I looked from one to another and took a deep breath.

"Please," I interrupted. "I need to get the story from just one of you at a time. Why don't you begin at the beginning," I requested of Brenda.

I knew I would have trouble deciphering the story from three people talking at the same time, but I soon learned this was going to be the pattern for our whole attorney-client relationship. Even when I called their house, they would all get on different phones and talk at once. Ultimately they ended up disputing the facts among themselves while I listened.

"I bought my dog from Rita Lorree," Brenda began, but her mother interjected,

"Rita is a recognized breeder of standard poodles."

"She's very good at it," her father assured me in his comment.

"Please," I begged. "Let Brenda tell it."

"Rita told me she was going to be at the dog show in Denver, so I took Elliot, my standard poodle, to the show. I wasn't going to show him because he is only thirteen months old, but I needed to socialize him and I wanted Rita to see him."

"We had no idea what was going to happen," her mother interrupted again.

"Absolutely none," her father chorused.

I was going to have to decipher the story, I now realized, and nodded.

Brenda continued, "When we got to the show, Rita asked us to bring Elliot out near her trailer so she could watch his gait. She asked if she could trot him and I agreed. Rita and Elliot began trotting across the parking lot and back again. My mother and I were watching them. The next time she circled us she trotted him across the lot and suddenly the door to a van opened, and Rita, with Elliot on his leash, jumped in."

"They just drove away," Mrs. Harrison added, unable to keep silent even for a few minutes.

"Without doubt," the father added.

I felt fascinated by this dramatic story. Despite the confusion, it sounded like a plot for a *Murder, She Wrote* episode.

Brenda was getting more and more agitated, and the details spilled out in short bursts. "My mother and I were in shock at first because we had no idea what was happening. Then we realized that Rita was stealing Elliot! We ran to our car and began to chase her. We chased her for more than seventy miles to Fort Collins until the van pulled into a garage and closed the door. We then called the local police from the house next door. The police told us that because Elliot had been stolen in Denver we would have to call the Denver Police Department. We did. They told us to come back to Denver to file a report. While we were gone, Rita left the house in Fort Collins and drove to Texas. Now she has my dog in Texas and I want him back." Finally she took a breath.

"That's quite a story," I said sympathetically. "But why did she take the dog?" I questioned.

"I have a co-ownership agreement with her and she claims that the dog is not being handled properly for show purposes," Brenda answered.

"But she hasn't had a chance yet," Mrs. Harrison jumped in.

"Not a chance," the father echoed.

I stifled a smile. "Have you asked for the dog back?" I questioned Brenda.

"Yes, but she has refused," my three visitors answered simultaneously. I could see I was going to have to get used to the three of them answering every question at the same time.

I read over the co-ownership agreement. It provided that the dog had to be shown until he obtained a championship. It also stated that, if the dog was mistreated, Rita Lorree, the breeder, would have a right to repossess the dog. Even if the breeder had been able to prove that Brenda had mistreated the dog, she still would have to have taken legal channels to execute the repossession part of the contract. Rita couldn't simply "steal" the dog. I didn't think there was any chance that Brenda or her parents had in any way mistreated this dog. It appeared that this owner was new to showing, and the breeder knew this when she sold the dog to Brenda. Rita had put in the contract that the dog should not be shown until it was two years old, and yet she was now claiming that the dog wasn't going to be able to obtain a championship when he was only thirteen months old.

"You haven't yet breached the contract," I said, "and therefore there are no grounds for replevin by the breeder."

"Oh, I'm so glad." Brenda gave a sigh of relief.

"What a relief," said her mother, picking up on her expression.

"Oh yes," said the father.

I filed a complaint in replevin in Denver District Court. In Colorado, replevin actions are required to be filed in district court regardless of the value of the property being recovered even though district court is usually reserved for cases of a value in excess of ten thousand dollars. I immediately received a temporary order granting Brenda Harrison custody of Elliot pending a hearing on the right of ownership. The order was sent to the sheriff's department in Texas. Brenda and Mr. Harrison drove through the night to Texas to retrieve Elliot. The breeder refused to turn the dog over. The Texas sheriff told the Harrisons they would need to get the Colorado order transferred to a State of Texas court. They came back to Colorado and I filed for a transfer of the replevin order to Texas. In the meantime, the case had been set for trial.

At the trial Rita appeared by telephone from Texas. We presented the evidence of ownership, which was primarily the contract, the canceled checks for payment of Elliot, veterinary records for Elliot, and photographs of Elliot with Brenda. Rita argued, "The dog is not fit to be shown and never will be unless I have custody of it. The dog will have to be in my possession until he turns two years old, and then I will show the dog myself. Otherwise, he will never get a championship as required in the contract."

Because the two years had not yet come and because Brenda had not even had a chance to try to perform the requirements of the contract, I argued, "The showability of the dog is not at issue. The contract has yet to be performed. Without a breach of contract, there is no ground for repossession."

Judge Harlow's white eyebrows looked starched as he informed us, "I'm in a hurry to get back to my million-dollar business cases. Agreed. The Harrisons get custody of the dog."

The family then traveled back to Texas to retrieve their dog.

Upon execution of the order in favor of the Harrisons, the Texas sheriff's department with Brenda along entered Rita's home.

"I refuse to turn over Elliot," she said, kicking and screaming at the officers when Brenda entered calling for Elliot. Rita smacked Brenda. Finally the officers restrained Rita. The Harrisons got the dog and immediately left the state.

Once back in Colorado, though, simple custody did not mean much to the Harrisons. Now they had to try to show Elliot to get a championship, and they feared that at every dog show they would meet Rita or people working for her. They might steal Elliot again. When they told me about their fears, I tried to reassure them. "At least you have two years to comply with the co-ownership contract, and you have Elliot."

In fact, I was right, because Elliot was a superb animal and Brenda a quick learner as a handler. He was soon placing at shows. They invited me to join them at one, and sure enough he received a blue ribbon!

I soon learned that all replevin actions for dogs have an aura of mystery about them. I next received a call from Ferdinand and Eliza Dante, a good-looking couple in their late thirties, who had had their dogs taken from them. They had adopted a male greyhound they named Dog through a greyhound adoption agency. After they had Dog for a few months, they thought he was lonely, so they adopted a female greyhound they called Little Girl. The greyhound adoption agencies were established as a means of finding homes for retired racing greyhounds. Because so many greyhounds are bred for racing and so few are active racers, there are a lot of racers without jobs, and therefore without homes. Rather than have all of these dogs put to sleep, agencies exist across the country to try to place these dogs in good homes. One critical part of the adoption is to ensure that the dog is spayed or neutered so that more greyhounds aren't added to the unwanted dog population.

Before the Dantes had adopted Dog and Little Girl, they'd filled out an extensive questionnaire regarding their lifestyles and commitment to the dogs and agreed that the spaying or neutering would be done within three months of adoption. It also specified a variety of other things concerning how the dog was to be treated, including wearing a collar at all times, receiving exercise and training, and other less critical performances than the requirement that the dogs not be bred. The contract ended by stating that the agency had the right to repossess the dog in the event *any* of the requirements was violated.

The Dantes came to me visibly upset. "We scheduled the dogs to be neutered," Eliza said in a trembling voice. "But not knowing when they were going to be in heat, the dogs had bred before we had a chance to have the surgeries performed. The next thing we knew, we had a litter of nine greyhound puppies."

Ferdinand took up for his tearful wife. "We loved the dogs and the puppies, and we promised to find good homes for all of the puppies. Nonetheless, Kent Walker, the director of the adoption agency, came to our home while we both were working and, in front of our twelve-year-old daughter, Jana, they forcibly removed Dog and Little Girl and the nine puppies from our home. When they left, the agency posted their court order for possession on the door."

After hearing the whole story, I believed the Dantes had not intended the breeding and I believed they had suffered as a result of the repossession of the dogs.

"The taking of the family pets from a crying twelve-year-old is an assault on the child, and I'm not about to let such a horrific thing happen," I told them.

At the hearing for custody pending trial, I argued, "The repossession is invalid because the contract is too vague. Under the terms of the contract, a repossession could also be had if the collar was removed from the dog. The requirements were not specifically stated as being grounds for repossession and therefore the agency was wrong to repossess the dogs without warning."

Eliza was sniffling, and I paused to give her a sympathetic look. Then I continued, "These nine puppies and their parents should not be forced to remain kenneled when they could be in their home with the family that loves them."

That is when Judge Harrington banged her gavel and shouted from the bench, "I will not have these dogs treated as though this is a custody case. It is not. It is a case for possession of property."

In hearing that their beloved dogs were considered property, the Dantes burst into tears. I felt sorry for them, but what I didn't know was what good actors they were. After the preliminary hearing when it was determined that the dogs would stay at the agency's kennel until trial, I learned from the prosecutor that my clients were not as innocent or devoid of manipulative motives as they seemed. Not only had Dog been bred to Little Girl, the adopted female, but the Dantes had "found" another female greyhound and they now had another litter of greyhound puppies at home, also sired by Dog. I called my clients and told them to come to my office right away.

"This is where I throw in the towel," I told them. "It is hard enough defending dog owners who have been wronged, but, if clients lie about the facts of a case, there is no chance of defending them properly. I'm not taking this case to trial, and that's final."

Though Ferdinand and Eliza brought their daughter to the office and put on a crying act which could have earned them a prize, I ushered them out.

My next client, Laura Downing, a breeder of Rottweilers, was much more open, but she also had not adhered to proper legal procedure. Downing explained, "I reclaimed a female dog I sold to Rita Nallier because she was mistreated and neglected."

She took out photographs of a very emaciated and bruised Rottweiler named Coco and passed them to me. I gasped.

The case had originally been filed in small claims court. Downing had answered the complaint and counter claimed for damages to Coco. Because of the counter claim, Nallier had hired attorney Rob Dalton to represent her, thereby moving the case to county court.

"I feel I should also have an attorney, which I can't really afford."

"Well, I can't stand to see animals abused. I'll take the case and keep the costs low."

In county court there is no exchange of evidence. Dalton did not know that I had photos of a very emaciated dog taken the day Coco had been picked up from Nallier. He did not know that I had a veterinarian's opinion as to the ill-health of Coco at the time Downing retrieved Coco from Nallier. I was prepared to use this evidence to show that the repossession had been done pursuant to a contract that permitted repossession for abuse or neglect of the dog. The veterinarian's statements would also show that my client had suffered expenses in excess of sale price of Coco in bringing the dog back to good health.

When we appeared for the trial, Laura had six witnesses with her, and I brought Jerry who'd again acted as my pet detective. Nallier and her attorney had brought three witnesses. A case that had originally been intended as small claims was turning into a hotly contested trial.

When I arrived at the courthouse, Dalton asked that we discuss the case away from the witnesses and clients. We entered a conference room off the courtroom.

"Look," he proceeded to tell me, "my client is entitled to compensation for the loss of Coco to Downing." Nallier didn't even want Coco back, only money. Knowing that Dalton would not have time to call a veterinarian to present evidence contradicting the evidence of our veterinarian, I revealed our evidence. Without time to discredit the veterinarian or to counter his testimony, I knew my client's position was so much stronger that Nallier didn't have a chance.

Dalton sat back mulling over my evidence and then said, "I guess we have to try the case."

"I'm ready," I responded too eagerly. "Let's go."

"Oh, we won't be trying the case today," he informed me, his voice taking a superior air. "The judge isn't here."

I blew up. "What do you mean, the judge isn't here?"

"She had to go to give a speech," he informed me, as if that was the usual practice for a judge.

It was a lesson in not being overconfident. He had known we weren't going to trial but I hadn't. He now had time to obtain evidence to counter all of my "surprise" evidence. I knew my client's case would be greatly prejudiced by any delay in the trial. I had to move quickly and I knew it.

"We'll get another judge," I told him decisively.

"I don't think anyone else is available," he responded.

I was quite sure he was hoping no other judge was available, but I wasn't about to take that excuse.

"We'll find someone," I insisted as I hurriedly left the conference room. I told Jerry what had happened.

"Do you want me to get you a judge?" he asked. As always, he was ready to move mountains for me.

"Yes," I replied, not knowing what he had in mind. "Find me anyone; we have to try this case today."

He disappeared as I explained to my upset client what was happening. Although Laura didn't understand that her case may have been prejudiced by my revealing the evidence I had wanted to keep confidential, she did know that all of her witnesses would have to return and that the cost of her case would now double since we would have to prepare again for trial and appear again.

Time inched by as I waited for Jerry. Then I breathed a sigh of relief as I heard him calling me.

"Linda," Jerry said. "I'm in the clerk's office. I need you here."

Walking over, the clerk said, "The judge has gone to give a speech."

Jerry winked at me over her bent head and motioned he was taking off. I wasn't happy being left there alone but had no choice.

"Gone to give a speech?" I said incredulously. "I have six witnesses out there waiting to appear at a trial. I have a client who thought her case was in small claims court and is now paying double attorney fees to reappear," I said, nearly shouting. "And the judge just up and went to give a speech"

"She's introducing one of the justices of the Colorado Supreme Court," the clerk told me, as if that explained everything.

"I don't care if she's introducing the President of the United States; she can't do it when we have a trial about to begin."

"We meant to call you," the clerk said meekly.

All of the other office workers began clearing the room to let the clerk deal with me. Jerry had disappeared. Dalton was hiding in a corner. No one ever questions a judge's actions, but I was fed up with the attitude of judges that a dog case was not a real case. I had a very real client who was suffering because the judge had wanted to give an important speech.

"I'm sorry, but we will have to reschedule the trial," the clerk continued.

"Wait a minute," I said in disgust as I exited the office.

Jerry came running up to me and said, "Come here. I want you to talk to the presiding judge."

While I had been arguing with the clerk, he had found the presiding judge and told him of our dilemma. Now I was not angry anymore. I was scared. What would the presiding judge have to say about all this? Maybe I should have acquiesced to the clerk's order and rescheduled the trial. Fighting with judges was not one of my favorite activities. But now I had no choice so I followed Jerry to the judge's office.

"Good afternoon, Ms. Cawley," Judge Morris addressed me in his deep sonorous voice, already knowing my name.

I wondered if this was a funeral dirge.

"Good afternoon, Your Honor," I responded. Now I was the meek one.

"Have a seat," he instructed. "Your investigator here tells me you have a problem with one of my judges?"

I didn't like the way that was worded. I was sure I was going to get reamed for questioning the authority of the court.

"Your Honor," I said defensively, "I have a client who was originally a defendant in a small claims case. The plaintiff moved the case to county court and my client was forced to hire counsel. We are ready for trial. We have six witnesses with us today, and no judge."

"I understand the judge was called away at the last minute to an important meeting."

I didn't know if he was being sarcastic, but I knew the reason for our scheduled judge not being on the bench was not the issue. The fact was, she was not on the bench for a scheduled trial.

"You were not informed that the judge was unavailable?"

"No, Your Honor," I answered quietly.

"Then I think you are right in being upset," I was surprised to hear him say. "I will talk to the judge when she returns. In the meantime, I am available to hear your case if you are ready to proceed."

I was shocked. Herbert Morris, the presiding judge, the director of all other judges, was agreeing to hear a dog case at the last minute.

"Thank you, Your Honor. That will be wonderful," I said, meaning it.

By the time I returned to the courtroom, Rob Dalton had heard who would be hearing the case. He and his client immediately agreed that Laura could keep Coco and they would pay the medical expenses.

A couple of days later, I received a call from a very apologetic judge who wanted to state on the record her reasons for being absent. They weren't very good and she knew it, but she needed to protect herself. For some reason, she had been led to believe that I was going to file a grievance on her. I had never stated that I would do such a thing and never did, but nonetheless she thought I would. For that reason, I made every effort to avoid her courtroom.

13

Arrested for Barking Back at a Barking Dog

"I've been charged with cruelty to animals," graying and paunchy Steve Stark told me as he sat in my office in his blue Postal Service uniform which matched his honest-looking, gray-blue eyes.

My first thought was that the charges must have something to do with his job. Maybe he kicked a dog that was coming at him, or threw his mailbag at a dog.

"What did you do?" I asked.

"Believe me, Ms. Cawley, nothing any normal person wouldn't have done under the circumstances. I was out on my back porch hanging my laundry. The neighbor's dog is always barking, and that afternoon he was barking at me louder than usual. He was giving me a headache, so, to get away, I walked inside. The sound came through the walls. I flipped on the television. But the barking was so loud it was driving me crazy. So I called animal control. I had called them previously about this dog, so they knew what the situation was. They told me they would be right over," Stark said, mopping the perspiration from his face and pausing for a moment.

He continued, "I went back outside to hang more laundry, but the dog was still barking. So," he paused and looked at me, a definite sad-eyed dog look, "I barked back at him. He went 'ruff-ruff-ruff,' and I," here his face became red and high-colored, "went 'ruff-ruff-ruff yourself,'" Stark said as he demonstrated his facility at the activity.

I stifled a laugh and said, "Go on."

"Well, the next thing I knew animal control officers are standing in my yard saying I was cruel to the dog because I had been barking at him. I told them that he had been barking at me first. But that didn't cut no mustard, so they charged me with cruelty to animals," he concluded.

I shook my head. I couldn't believe the city attorney was really going forward with such a case.

Later, I went to the courthouse and pulled the prosecutor's file on the case. Their evidence was the testimony of a neighbor who lived behind the dog owner. She said she'd seen Stark out on his back porch, scratching and pawing the ground. When she went out in her backyard to check further, she heard a man, as she said, just barking and called animal control. Her call had come in just after Stark's call to animal control complaining about a barking dog. When animal control arrived at Stark's house to investigate, they charged him with cruelty to animals.

The law in Carol City where Stark lives reads, "One commits cruelty to animals when he performs such acts that inflict pain, constitute neglect or harassment of an animal."

The prosecutor's contention was that Steve Stark's barking constituted "harassment" to the dog.

I called the city attorney and said, "You can't be serious about this charge."

"We are very serious about this," the young attorney responded curtly.

"Why?" I asked. "Mr. Stark was merely barking back at a barking dog. You have numerous complaints on file that this dog had been barking previously. There are witnesses that this dog was barking this time. And yet you feel you have enough evidence that my client's barking constituted cruelty?"

Mike McClure, the city attorney, wouldn't budge. He wouldn't even offer a plea to a lesser charge, although I couldn't think what type of lesser charge I would permit my client to take for having barked.

"You know," I said. "We also have a freedom of speech issue here. This man is being prosecuted for the 'content' of his speech, a violation of his First Amendment rights."

"That's not the way we see it," McClure responded. The young city attorney was adamant. "We're going to move forward."

We went to arraignment. I told Stark I really didn't think there was a chance the judge would let this type of case get past him at arraignment. I was wrong. The judge allowed the case to stand for trial.

After reviewing and discarding several strategies, I felt I had no choice then but to take this case to the press. With animal cases, the courts are often so negative towards the subject matter that the cases never get a fair trial in court.

I have found that public opinion is often against legal opinion and can be a great deciding factor. "The concept of using taxpayers' money to charge a man with cruelty to animals for barking back at a barking dog seems quite unjust," I said to the reporter the news service sent to interview me. When he started to laugh, I knew I was in trouble.

I had one more strategy. "Jerry," I said to my much beleaguered and loyal husband, "I. . . ."

He interrupted. "You have that look in your eye," he said and sighed, by then knowing me both wisely and too well.

"It's the Stark case."

He nodded.

"Our only good shot as I see it is if we can show the dog and my client aren't enemies."

"They seem to speak the same language if that's a consolation."

"Darling," I said, musing, "if we could get a video of Steve and the dog 'talking'"—Jerry frowned—"or something," I said. "Would you?"

He shook his head. "I'll give it a try."

It merely seemed comical to the press. The newspaper coverage did nothing to sway the city attorney. They liked their case and they were going to take it to trial. Fortunately, no one requested a jury trial. I really couldn't see putting twelve people through a day of listening to testimony over a barking man's guilt or innocence.

On Monday, with the press in attendance, the trial began.

Carol Riordan, the neighbor who'd observed my client barking, was the first witness. She was a tall, mid-fortyish woman with very short brown hair and glasses. "I saw Steve

Stark in his yard, and I heard the dog barking," she said. "I went outside to investigate." She added, "I heard him barking at the dog."

"Could you describe what you heard?" the prosecutor asked.

"Yes," she responded. "He went 'ruff-ruff.'"

"And what did the dog do?" the prosecutor continued.

"He went 'ruff-ruff,' too," the witness replied.

This was going to be great. I couldn't wait to cross-exam this witness. Was she sure it was "ruff-ruff" and not "bow-wow-wow?"

First, I cross-examined her on her ability to see my client.

"I saw him in the yard."

"Would you look at these?" I said, placing five photographs into evidence. "These are photographs which indicate that the location where Stark had been standing in his yard could not have been visible from your yard."

After questioning, Mrs. Riordan admitted that she didn't see him but had only heard him.

"And how were you able to identify that it was the defendant?" I asked.

"I recognized his voice," she answered, attempting to reestablish some credibility.

"Had you heard him bark before?" I challenged her, while the courtroom erupted into gales of laughter.

"Quiet in the court," Judge Henry said sternly, but I saw the hint of a smile at the corners of his mouth as he gave everyone an extra few minutes to recover.

"Well, no." She hesitated. "But I knew it was him."

The next witness to testify was the dog's owner, Barbara Apprighano. "My dog was upset when I came home," she testified, "and that is when my neighbor told me that the defendant had been barking at my poor Cecil."

Poor Cecil was a Great Dane so, in my opinion, if anyone should have been terrified it should have been my client.

"When you say 'upset,'" I began my cross-examination, "could you describe how your dog acted?"

"He was very nervous," she responded, pulling her glasses on and off. "Like someone had hurt him."

"Did he act afraid of the defendant and his house?" I asked, leading the witness where I needed her to go.

"Yes," she responded, taking the bait. "He won't ever go near the fence on that side."

"Judge Henry," I said. "I request permission to show a videotape."

The judge, much to his credit, complied. A videotape machine on a cart was pushed into the courtroom. Dramatically, I flipped the switch on. The tape rolled, showing Steve Stark playing with the dog from across the fence that bordered the two properties. This dog was friendly towards my client and certainly not afraid of him, I pointed out as the tape played.

Then I called Steve Stark to the stand.

After swearing him in and asking a few standard questions, I moved to the day of the incident.

"What did you do?" I asked him.

"The dog was barking," he said. "I was outside hanging my laundry, and I barked back at him."

"How did you bark?" I questioned.

"Do you want me to demonstrate?" he asked me.

"Yes." I nodded, hoping he wouldn't be too graphic. Of course, we had role-played this and other questions. But

I'd been in enough courtroom situations to know that most of the time, even if a witness is prepared for what's coming, the drama of the moment often stimulates an impromptu performance. And I guessed correctly.

Steve Stark got down on all fours.

I shielded my eyes, knowing what was coming next and trying to keep a poker face.

"I went 'ruff-ruff-ruff yourself,'" Steve animatedly answered as he demonstrated how he had barked.

Once again the courtroom erupted in laughter, and the judge banged his gavel down to get silence.

So it had been ruff-ruff-ruff, not bow-wow-wow. We closed our case. The judge ruled not guilty and we all went home.

14

Cruel or Cool

I would have thought the lengthy and expensive process of the Stark case would have dampened the city attorney's desire to prosecute cruelty to animals cases for harassment. But it didn't.

Only a few weeks later, I had another call from the same jurisdiction.

"Hello," a gravelly voice on the other end of the telephone said. "I'm Lou Watkins and I need to know if it's a crime to walk a dog from a pickup truck?"

I needed more information. "Have you been charged with a crime?" I asked him.

"I think so," he responded hesitantly. "I have here a citation for cruelty to animals, but, you have to believe me," he went on, "I wasn't being cruel."

"Where do you live?" I questioned him.

"Carol City," he answered as I released a sympathetic murmur.

"What were you doing?" I asked him.

"I have an English Setter. Max injured his leg a few months back, and our veterinarian told me I had to walk him every day to get the leg back into shape. Max is two years old; I'm seventy-eight years old. I can't walk like I used to. My veterinarian told me to just very slowly drive in my pickup truck and let Max walk along behind the truck. My grandson sits in the back of the truck and holds Max's leash because we have a leash law here in Carol City. Well, last Tuesday I was driving the truck and a motorcycle copy came up behind me and pulled me over. He charged me with cruelty to animals."

This sounded like something that would happen in Carol City and Mr. Watkins sounded anything but cruel. His walking the dog from the truck wasn't done to be cruel, but rather to promote the health of the dog. I called the city attorney, and this time he agreed to drop the charges if we could get a letter from Mr. Watkins's veterinarian. We did, and the charges were dropped.

Another case soon came in from Mrs. Paula Roman who owned a white toy poodle. The animal control officer who issued the ticket for neglect had never seen a poodle with long hair. Mrs. Roman didn't like her dog clipped so she had let its coat grow out. The dog's veterinarian stated that the dog was in good health, he just had a long coat. The case was dismissed.

Among other abuse charges, the charge of serious cruelty to animal cases can be brought against owners who leave their pets in their cars on hot days. Dogs left in cars can die quickly as a result of heat prostration. In truth, dogs should not be in cars on hot days, and should never be left in the car with the windows rolled up or without water.

However, many caring pet owners take their dogs on errands with them and leave them in their parked vehicles for short periods of time.

Karen Nelson called me after she had been charged with cruelty to animals in the City of Denver when her golden retriever, Cody, was found by an attendant alone in Karen's car in the parking lot of a hospital where Karen usually worked as a nurse. The windows were cracked, but there was no water for Cody. Karen had stopped by the hospital to run inside and get her paycheck. To be sure the dog was comfortable Karen had parked the car with Cody in it under a tree. While she was in the hospital, an emergency had arisen and she had been detained. She returned about thirty minutes later to find the car surrounded by police officers and Cody standing outside. Even though the officers had offered Cody water, he hadn't drunk any and didn't appear to be in any distress. Though it had been a cool sixty degrees that day and Karen was only gone a half hour, nonetheless Karen was charged with cruelty. However, once I was able to establish the temperature and that the car had been in the shade, the city attorney agreed to drop the charges.

In a similar case I had in California, Marge Burlington had been charged with cruelty to animals by the Beverly Hills Police. She had parked her car with her poodle, Victor, still in the car inside of a parking structure on Rodeo Drive. The windows had been cracked and the outside temperature was about seventy degrees.

A passerby saw the dog in the car and broke the window to let the dog out. He then called the police who were at the car when Mrs. Burlington returned. They charged her with cruelty to animals.

"How long was the dog in the car?" I questioned her.

"Only ten minutes," she answered.

"How are you sure of that?" I inquired.

"Because the parking garage gives you a ticket with a stamp of the time on it and it was stamped at ten-oh-seven. My citation from the police is for ten-fifteen," she answered.

"Do you still have the ticket?" I asked hopefully.

"Of course," she replied. "I thought I had lost the ticket in all of the commotion and paid the attendant for the whole day. But later I found that ticket."

"That's good," I congratulated her.

I called the city attorney and told him we could prove that the dog was only in the car for ten minutes or less and the temperature inside of the car in the garage when it was seventy degrees outside with the windows cracked would not have ever gotten so hot as to injure the dog. The city attorney, impressed by the proof, agreed to drop the charges. The passerby had meant well, but he had no idea of the real facts on how long Mrs. Burlington had been gone when he came upon the dog.

Owners can show good intentions if the dog really wasn't at any risk because the temperature was not more than seventy degrees and the car was parked in the shade. In these cases, the charges are usually dropped or a reprimand given.

Many times a lack of knowledge of dogs can be the cause for charges against an owner to be issued. Most people who have dogs love them and often the owner knows more about the breed and her dog than the well-meaning passerby who calls the police. This is often the case with breeders and show people who tend to keep their pets in airline kennels while traveling. Although I have had clients charged with cruelty for confining their pets, kennels are not only the safest way for dogs to travel, but also are a comfort to a dog when on the road.

The difficulty with cruelty cases beyond real abuse such as starvation or beating is determining what is cruel and what is merely a different way of treating a pet than another person would prefer. I have actually had co-ownership agreement disputes because dogs were left outside at night, outside during the day, sleeping in garages, sleeping in basements, not being fed high-protein food, being fed high-protein food, not being shown, being shown too often. It is always a matter of opinion as to what is right for the dog.

I do not believe the law should intrude in telling an owner how to care for his pet unless there are signs of abuse.

In a case that I felt developed my sense of purpose for dog law, I was called by Harriet Barnes, representative of the Women's Animal Shelter League. "We need you to represent our group in obtaining custody of a purebred dog that is at the local animal control."

The story began when Homer Trent, a transient, was arrested for loitering by sleeping on the beach. He had his Irish setter with him. Trent went to jail, the dog to animal control. On discovering that the dog was owned by this transient, the Women's Animal Shelter League moved in to prevent the dog from being returned to her owner. Harriet further explained, "We have to stop the tragedy of this wonderful Irish setter's life on the streets."

Even I who love dogs was amazed at their sympathy for the dog and lack of it for her master. Further, it was apparently their opinion that only the wealthy and well-to-do should be able to own purebred dogs. Even if Homer had no home, they felt the dog should have one. However, I believed then and still do that a dog's home is with its master. If a man is homeless, then his loyal and beloved dog will be homeless too, but certainly the dog should not be taken away from him because the dog is not able to sleep in comfortable surroundings.

One of the most critical things about the attachment of a dog and owner is the intense quality of that love despite the circumstances. A dog is a great animal for that reason. A dog's loyalty is to her master, whether rich or poor, smart or dumb, a homeowner or homeless, and it is that loyalty that makes the dog such a great animal. It is also that loyalty and dedication to its owner that is the essence of dog law. Dog laws should protect the dog owner's emotional bond with his pet. The dog laws should allow a person to invest emotionally in a pet without forcing the destruction of that bond. To take a dog away from a master because the master is homeless violates the integrity of the human/dog relationship. The dog doesn't care whether it has a house to live in. I couldn't agree with the Women's Animal Shelter League that all dogs should live in comfortable homes because I believe all dogs should be loved and live with the one who loves them, regardless of the person's economic circumstances. I refused to represent them.

15

Arrest that Dog on Sight

"When I go to a dog show in Wyoming, I have to drive through three cities that prohibit my purebred American Staffordshire terrier," Lisa Jennings told me while I was giving a lecture on dog law to a Colorado Springs dog club. "I'm concerned that if I just stop at a traffic light, they could arrest me and take my dog."

These concerns are legitimate when it comes to breed specific legislation. In 1989 the City of Denver passed a law prohibiting "pit bulls" from the city. Pit bulls that had been in Denver prior to the law could stay so long as they were registered with animal control. The law was immediately challenged as unconstitutional by the Colorado Dog Fancier's Association. They lost. They appealed and lost again. The law was deemed constitutional, and is now a valid law in Denver.

A pit bull or a dog which an animal control officer suspects to be at least 50 percent pit bull can be taken from its owner on sight. This means that the dog can be retrieved from a backyard or from the inside of a home. Roberta Singleton couldn't believe it could possibly be legal when the police came to her home and told her that they would be taking her dog, Teddy, because they suspected he was a pit bull. In fact, Teddy was a pit bull but Roberta had failed to register the dog as required by the law because she hadn't trusted the law then. She certainly didn't trust it now. She called me while holding the police at bay on her front step.

"The police are here and they say they will take my dog," Roberta screamed into the phone.

"What kind of dog is it?" I questioned.

"He's a pit bull, but I never registered him as a pit bull," she explained. "So now they say they can take him."

"Does he look like a pit bull?" I questioned her.

"Yes, but they can't take him. He's a good dog," she replied.

I explained to her the legal grounds the police had for taking her dog on sight if it looked like a pit bull, even if it wasn't a pit bull, and she was even admitting it was. "They can take her, but you will have the right to fight their determination in court," I told her. She was not appeased.

"It will be over my dead body that they take this dog," she cried hysterically.

I had to inform her that was a distinct possibility. The police had a legal right to take the dog and her stopping them would be an obstruction of justice. As unfair as it seemed, once a breed specific ban becomes law, there is nothing an owner can do to prevent the dog from being taken from the home. They then have to fight the legal determination that the dog is the breed specified. Breed ban cases can be very difficult because there is seemingly no recourse for the owner of the breed which has been banned.

Under constitutional law, a person has a right to a hearing before there can be a deprivation of property. Because the taking of a dog is a deprivation of property, the owner is entitled to a hearing. In the Denver case, the hearing was similar to the vicious dog court system in San Diego. A veterinarian acts as the judge, the animal control or police officer who picked up the dog acts as the prosecution, and the owner has the burden of proving that the dog is not a pit bull.

The evidence that the dog is a pit bull is the officer's testimony. That testimony is based solely upon his or her personal opinion that the dog "looks like" a pit bull. In order for owners to prove otherwise, they must have breeding records establishing the dog's non-pit bull heritage. This means at least 51 percent of the dog's blood-lines must be from a non-pit bull source. Usually dogs that get picked up are mixed breeds and the owner has no proof of the dog's lineage. Even if the owner never knew the dog had any pit bull in him, they might not be able to prove that the dog is really a boxer mix or Labrador mix, each of which can resemble a pit bull.

Because the breed of pit bull has never been specifically defined, dog fancier associations have challenged these laws on the vagueness of the description. Without a more specific description, they argue, the law is too vague to enforce. The courts have found otherwise and have allowed such laws to be passed.

There are precedents for such decisions. In England, the breed Japanese tosa was banned from even being permitted into the country. An unknowing breeder had her dog shipped into England. In quarantine it was discovered that the dog was a Japanese tosa. The quarantine officials prevented the dog from being released to the owners. Because the breed was not permitted in the country, the owners had no place to put the dog. They requested that the dog be permitted to be shipped out of the country. Officials, not knowing what their responsibility was, refused. The dog was trapped in an administrative quagmire for months, living in quarantine kennels and prevented from entering or leaving England. Ultimately the dog was shipped into Europe, after great frustration and expense to his owners.

The best defense to a breed specific law is to prevent the law from being enacted in the first place. In general, vicious dog laws can be drafted so as to protect the public against vicious dogs of any breed, not to vaguely target one breed over another.

Other new laws that can be frustrating for the dog owner are those that limit who can breed their dogs. Because of the proliferation of unwanted dogs, communities are concerned about reckless breeding. Limiting who can breed dogs is an infringement of one's rights that must be drafted so as to be constitutional. The breed ban must therefore have some relationship to the problem at hand. The most enforceable breeding bans are those that are designed to prevent careless breeding which result in unwanted puppies who end up being put to sleep by animal control, which costs the community money. By charging breeders to obtain a license to breed, the community is able to recoup some of the cost of caring for and destroying the unwanted puppies and breeders at least are able to breed dogs if they pay the fee. The trend is for animal shelters not to release any pet that has not been neutered or spayed, and to require breeders to pay for a license to breed. Usually city dog licenses are also more expensive for those who do not alter their pets.

Breeders not only need to obtain the necessary license to be able to breed their dogs, but they may also be subject to a lemon law. The lemon laws generally require breeders to sell healthy dogs. They do so by imposing guarantees on the sale of puppies from breeders who are subject to the laws because they sell a specified number of puppies per year. If the puppy they sell develops a genetic defect, the breeder may be required to compensate the buyer as much as double the cost of the dog in medical bills, or offer a replacement puppy at no charge. Because many breeders get around their own contractual hereditary defect guarantees by requiring that the defective dog be returned before a replacement dog will be given, something they know most owners cannot bear to do, they are not forced to perform their own guarantees. The lemon laws get around the contractual issues by requiring the breeder to compensate the owner without requiring that the sick dog be either returned to the breeder or put to sleep. Since breeding laws and lemon laws can be tough on small breeders, they usually only apply to breeders who sell a large number of dogs.

A new type of dog law case developed from case law rather than statute is called the wrongful birth action. Owners of female dogs have brought successful legal action against the owners of male dogs that have caused unwanted breeding of the female dog. In one celebrated case in South Carolina, a black Labrador retriever named Rocky escaped from his secured backyard by digging under a six-foot wooden fence, something he had never done before, and traveled across town where he smelled a female in heat. The female, a purebred golden retriever, had been contracted to be bred to another purebred golden retriever. The expensive breeding was apparently not going so well. However, while the male retriever stood by and watched, a horny Rocky jumped the female retriever's fence and was intimate with her. The female's owner, who was inside the house, ran outside and tried to separate the dogs. But they hadn't been separated early enough. The pregnancy went forward. The puppies were delivered a couple of months later, five yellow and five black. In a state of distress, the female golden's owner had her dog spayed, believing she was forever tainted from giving birth to purebred golden retrievers again. She then went after the Labrador's owner for all medical bills, the cost of birthing the puppies, and the loss of her female breed bitch, and won a judgment in excess of four thousand dollars. The case was being appealed when I was called to consult.

Dan Warren, the Labrador owner, argued that he wasn't the only one who had been negligent. He had restrained his dog, Rocky, but, "smelling a dog in heat was too much for him. He did just what came naturally," he said. "The breeder was negligent by not confining her female better." He also argued that the breeder had caused her own damages by spaying a breedable dog. "There was no evidence that the female needed to be spayed."

The two sides went back and forth arguing the negligence of the wrongful birth. By this time, homes had been found for all the puppies, but the case wasn't resolved. Because the expense of an appeal was too much for Dan Warren, who couldn't afford to pay the judgment, I found a creative way to settle the case: on *The Maury Povich Show*, where both owners appeared and the audience decided the verdict.—that love should triumph.

16

"Not in My Town You Don't"

Neighbors often get very alarmed when they hear the word "kennel." Visions of yapping dogs and distinctly unpleasant odors fill their heads and they invariably show up at hearings in a panic, and begin objecting.

There are ways of getting variances from zoning regulations but they can be tricky. A variance must be applied for with the local zoning commission, a group which usually likes the status quo. Even if you get over this hurdle, there are still those panicky neighbors to deal with.

Ray and Eva Moore lived in a covenanted community outside of Colorado Springs. I had first met the Moores a couple of years prior to their zoning issue when two of their small terriers had been killed by a neighbor's Rottweiler that had come onto the Moores' property. Mrs. Moore, a German immigrant who spoke little English, had witnessed the entire attack. Mr. Moore had beaten the Rottweilers off the smaller dogs with a shovel, to no avail. Both dogs had to be destroyed because of the severity of their injuries. At that time, the Moores had been contemplating a civil suit against the owners of the Rottweilers. I had met with Mr. Moore to discuss the case, but I never heard from them again. Now they were calling because the City of Colorado Springs had ordered that they get rid of their dogs.

Mrs. Moore was in a panic over losing the dogs, and Mr. Moore came to Denver to meet with me. Apparently to lessen her grief when she'd lost her first two dogs to the Rottweiler attack, Mrs. Moore had bought more. Now, instead of two dogs, the couple had eight dogs on the property. By law only three dogs were permitted per household. The Moores had already filed a request for a zoning variance. This had brought an onslaught of protest from the neighbors in their community who feared their neighborhood would become commercial if one household were permitted to have a "kennel" on the property. There was too much protest to have any success at the variance hearing, so Mr. Moore withdrew his request.

I sent Jerry down to Colorado Springs to investigate the neighborhood. He observed that all of the houses were on lots of at least one acre. Most of the homeowners had dogs and at the entrance to the property there were horses. It certainly was not too congested a community for dogs. But the neighbors were adamantly against the Moores keeping their terriers.

Jerry first spoke with Anna Lipton, the woman who headed the protest against the Moores' zoning variance petition. Mrs. Lipton was also of German descent and apparently not too friendly with Mrs. Moore.

"Why are you against the Moores' request for a zoning variance?" Jerry asked her after he had been invited into her home.

"Well, let me tell you," she began in her thick accent. "That woman does not need all those dogs. They bark and they run around the yard and make a mess of things. We don't need people like her in this neighborhood. This is a nice neighborhood and we want to keep it that way."

"But the dogs are kept inside nearly all day," Jerry defended the Moores. "Have you actually found them to be a nuisance?"

"I certainly have. So has everyone else in this neighborhood."

Jerry next interviewed the neighbor who owned the Rottweilers. Mr. Salinas, the Rottweilers' owner, only shrugged his shoulders and said, "I really don't want to get involved but my wife insists that we join those who are opposed to their variance."

"Why?" Jerry asked him.

"Because we don't need a kennel here, I guess," he offered none too persuasively. Jerry spoke with other neighbors only to hear the same sentiment voiced by Mr. Salinas. It seemed that the fear of a kennel was the basis for most of the neighbors' opposition, except for Mrs. Lipton who personally did not like Mrs. Moore. The only variance that would permit the Moores to own eight dogs on their property would be a rezoning to a classification that permitted kennels. The neighbors' fear was reasonable. An alternative approach would be to request a "permissive" grandfathering. By the city agreeing to grandfather the Moores' use of their property for eight dogs, they would be forever limited to the ownership of eight dogs and, as those dogs died, they would be required to reduce their dogs in number to the specified limit of three. If the neighbors did not protest the grandfathering, then no zoning variance would be necessary and no kennels would be permitted in the neighborhood. We scheduled a meeting at the community center in Colorado Springs for all neighbors to come and discuss this option.

It was a bitterly cold night that winter of 1994. As Jerry and I drove to Colorado Springs, a snowstorm developed, with sleet, heavy snow, and winds whipping up. We drove more than eighty miles to the meeting. Needless to say, very few people attended. The neighbors who did attend were the Liptons and Salinases. By the time we arrived at the meeting nearly twenty minutes late, Mrs. Lipton and Mrs. Moore were screaming at each other. Sometimes in English but mostly in German.

"Excuse me!" Jerry shouted into the mayhem of the room. "Attorney Linda Cawley is here on behalf of Mr. and Mrs. Moore. Maybe you would like to address your legal questions to her so the misunderstandings about this case can be resolved."

The room quieted down as everyone turned and faced me.

"Hello," I said softly, scared of what might transpire here. I really didn't want everyone directing their anger towards me. But they all sat glaring silently waiting for me to begin.

"I understand that your neighborhood is in opposition to the Moores' request for a zoning variance," I began, picking up momentum as I realized I had their attention. "It may be possible to resolve this problem without the Moores proceeding with their request."

I hesitated to see if I would be interrupted, but I was not. So I continued. "In many cases like this we are able to permit a dog owner to keep more than the limited number of dogs allowed by a city because they can be grandfathered under the old laws for the community. Although I realize that technically the Moores do not qualify to be grandfathered because they acquired their dogs after your neighborhood was annexed into the City of Colorado Springs, if the city does not object, they may be limited to owning the eight dogs they have right now if they agree not to acquire any more dogs and to reduce the number of dogs by natural attrition." The room stayed quiet. I was still waiting for them to start screaming at me in German. There was no response as they turned and looked at each other and shrugged.

"That's it," I told them so they would understand my proposal had been concluded.

"How would we know when the dogs die naturally that they didn't replace them with other dogs that look the same?" questioned Mrs. Lipton.

"We could record the license and identity of the dogs with the city and a veterinarian," I suggested.

"If they didn't follow the law before, why should we think they will follow this agreement now?" asked Mrs. Salinas.

"Because they are doing so to avoid your opposition at a zoning hearing. It is their desire to compromise with the neighborhood," I said on behalf of my clients.

"Oh no," started Mrs. Lipton. "This is just another way for them to get around the law. I don't trust them."

"We are honest people," Mrs. Moore jumped in.

"Eight dogs is too many. We don't want a kennel in the neighborhood," Mrs. Salinas joined in.

Tempers began rising again. I had to get control quickly.

"Wait a minute," I called out assertively. "If you don't agree to resolve this issue here tonight then the Moores will file a request for a variance and you will all have to appear at the hearing to protest the variance. If the variance is not granted, the Moores will continue pursuing other legal options and may keep this thing wrapped up with the city for years," I bluffed since I didn't really think the Moores had the wherewithal to keep this dispute going, nor would the city permit them, but we needed a resolution. "Not many neighbors are here tonight," I continued. "You are going to need a lot more support than this to oppose the variance."

"Let us talk with each other for a moment," Mr. Salinas requested. The Moores and Jerry and I left the room.

In the hallway Jerry rolled his eyes at me and indicated a hallway where we could talk out of earshot of the Moores. "What are you trying to do? You know they'll never win at a zoning board hearing."

"But don't you think the city would agree to grandfather the Moores just to avoid this mess?" I questioned him.

"Probably," Jerry agreed. "But this will be amazing if the neighbors agree to it."

The door opened and Mr. Salinas requested that we return to the meeting room.

It was quiet as we walked into the room, unlike our earlier entrance. Earlier the women had done all of the talking. Now it was the men who were speaking. Mr. Lipton began, "Do you think the city would accept the idea of grandfathering the Moores?"

"Yes, I do," I answered. "So long as there is no opposition from the neighbors."

"Then I believe we will consent to such a proposal so long as the Moores agree not to acquire any more dogs and to reduce the number of dogs they have as their dogs die." We had them. Now we had a resolution so long as it would be accepted by the city. We drove back to Denver late that night. The snow had stopped. The following day I spoke with the city attorney and he agreed to leave the Moores with eight dogs if we would agree not to pursue a zoning variance. Zoning variances are not easy to win so I was pleased with the outcome. It was not until nearly a year later that I had my first success with a zoning variance for a kennel within city limits.

Marshall Clifford had been hired from the Seattle Zoo to work at the Denver Zoo. One of the requirements of working for the zoo, which is owned by the city, is that all employees must live within city limits. Marshall was a noted breeder of a rare breed of dog, the Tibetan mastiff. Knowing Denver had a limit on the number of dogs, he searched for a property which would be compatible with his nine large dogs. The realtor had told him the property he found, with more than two acres of land, would permit such a use. The realtor had been wrong. Soon a neighbor complained about the large dogs, and Marshall was charged with having too many dogs. We applied for a zoning variance which would allow him to keep his dogs and breed one to two litters of puppies per year. Because zoning variances were rarely granted within the City of Denver, we needed an unusual tactic to get one.

Marshall suggested we bring one of his dogs to the hearing. Now I knew that dogs in the courtroom or at hearings can be unpredictable. They are in an unusual surrounding and one slip-up may destroy the whole case, so I hesitated. But in this case we needed everything we could find to help, and Marshall insisted the dog would be well-mannered.

Jerry had prepared the evidence by acquiring photographs of Marshall's property which had a double security system. If the dogs escaped from the inner kennel, they would be restrained by an outer kennel. It was the same system used by zoos to restrain their wild animals. The photographs also showed the distance between the properties and the way in which the kennels were hidden from all other properties and from the street.

We met Marshall and his dog Celeste outside of the City Building. She was a beautiful dog, large and long haired with a curled tail over her back. Her coat was dark brown and black with white markings on her face, and she had a wonderful personality. She greeted everyone with a "smile" and a wag of the tail and proceeded calmly into the building and into the boardroom where she curled up at Marshall's feet. She was so beautiful and polite that all of the board members kept petting her, rather than arguing why she shouldn't live in Denver.

Neighbors had complained because the Tibetan is a large, dominant-looking breed. But when the board members saw how gentle and polite this one was, there was no doubt in my mind the variance would be granted. Some of the board members even requested puppies from Celeste.

In most issues of zoning violations for an excessive number of dogs the best remedy is to avoid trouble. So long as neighbors do not complain, animal control does not usually interfere. Most complaints for excessive number of dogs come from utility company personnel and others on the property, not from the neighbors. People who own numerous dogs in excess of the number permitted by law are usually very tuned in to their neighbors.

When the zoning issues go beyond dogs into more exotic animals, I have had more trouble convincing animal control that the animals should be allowed to stay on the property. The breeder of Shiloh shepherds from whom I had purchased my new puppy, Tucker, must have suddenly decided that it would be nice to have a lion cub for her many dogs to wrestle with. Maggie purchased the cub, which she naturally named Leo, from a breeder in Ohio. Once the cub arrived in New York it settled nicely into its kennel alongside the numerous dogs. But trouble started when Leo contracted parvo and was rushed to the veterinarian. Fortunately, parvo is not deadly in lions as it can be with dogs, and Leo survived. But the veterinarian was forced to turn the cub over to animal control because they are illegal in the State of New York, something Maggie didn't know at the time she paid the breeder in Ohio.

In order to get Leo out of animal control I had to request a temporary restraining order from the local court preventing animal control from putting him to sleep. The judge in this small town in western New York had never handled a lion case before.

"What am I supposed to do with a lion?" he asked.

"My client just wants to keep the lion until she can apply for a wild animal permit," I told him.

"But I don't want a wild animal in my jurisdiction," he said almost jokingly.

"Then let her return the cub to Ohio where she purchased him, but don't let animal control put him to sleep," I begged him.

The judge agreed that the cub should not be put to sleep. But animal control didn't have the facilities to take care of him until Maggie received the necessary permits to keep the lion. So it was agreed that the cub would be returned to Ohio until the correct paperwork could be completed.

A couple of brown bears in Colorado were not so lucky. The jurisdiction did not permit the keeping of wild animals on private property. The bears were immediately confiscated and turned over to the Department of Wildlife before a restraining order could be granted. The trouble with these cases is what to do with the animals. The animal control departments are not set up for anything beyond dogs and cats and maybe a few rabbits. Relocation to a state where the animal is permitted is usually the best remedy. I have had to relocate wolves to Montana, bears to Canada, coveys to Australia, as well as the lion to Ohio.

One day, just after I found out I was pregnant, I received a call from the Aurora Animal Control asking me what they had to do with two pot-bellied pigs that had been dropped off during the night. The animal control group didn't even have food for them. Unlike dogs, there is no statute stating how long the animals must be held until they can be destroyed. Though I would have loved to take them, Jerry felt the anticipated baby was enough increase to our family at that time. But the likelihood of placing two pigs is not very high. Even if they were to try, how could animal control feed and care for them in a dog kennel until a new owner came along? Finally I thought of a novel solution. I set up a relationship with a local farmer where the pigs could stay while new homes were found.

Wolves and wolf hybrids are the most common wild animal problems. In some areas they are permitted, but even where they are not permitted it is difficult to identify which animals are wolf hybrids and which are merely "husky mixes." Two young men, Scott and Todd, both in their early twenties, came into my office one day after their two wolf hybrids, Shasta and Tundra, had been picked up for being "vicious" dogs. They had allegedly attacked a neighbor's small dog while they had been at large. The small dog had been seriously injured but had not died. Scott and Todd agreed to pay all veterinary expenses and apologized profusely to the owners of the dog. Their wolf hybrids had never gotten loose before. Todd lived in Montana with Shasta and had just been visiting his friend Scott who owned Tundra. Apparently, together Tundra and Shasta were trouble. The two hybrids had planned their escape. It was agreed that the charges would be dropped so long as the wolves were immediately moved to Montana. "In this case, as in some others," I explained to the two men, "removal of the problem to another jurisdiction can be the best solution." Todd and Scott couldn't get out of town quickly enough. They came to the courthouse with all of their things packed in their car or strapped to the top. Immediately after the hearing they went to animal control to get Tundra and Shasta out and hightailed it back to Montana.

17

Oodles of Poodles

We stood on the courthouse steps. "Is this, like, *101 Dalmatians*?" District Attorney Brett Holliday asked me. Although it had seemed very similar to a scene from a Disney movie when I had inspected the clients' house to determine whether I could actually represent someone who owned one hundred and four poodles, I couldn't let the prosecutor get away with making fun of the situation. I had been up against him in several other dog law cases and knew his reputation for winning at all costs.

"No," I responded. "These dogs don't have black spots." Keeping a light touch with dog cases is a necessity when dealing with prosecutors and other attorneys unfamiliar with dog law arguments. It is unique and sometimes humorous, which can often be turned to our advantage. Who would want to prosecute one hundred and one Dalmatians?

The Oodles of Poodles case might never have been mine at all.

Jerry and I were expecting our baby on August 16, 1994. I had a dog custody matter which was part of a divorce action scheduled for final disposition on August sixth. It was the earliest date I had been able to obtain. I was afraid to schedule the hearing after the baby was born since I didn't know when I would be able to return to work. The couple were arguing over their five-year-old golden retriever. I represented the wife, Susan Bellamy. By the time the trial neared, we believed a delay would be helpful to my client's position because it would give her ex-husband, Ken, more time to forget about the dog which was in her custody pending trial. However, toward the middle of July, my doctor advised me to slow down my work; so I moved the court for a continuance from the August sixth date.

The opposing attorney, Hank Riordan, argued that I was not in need of a continuance. "She has always known when the baby was due," he said. "That's just an excuse to delay the action."

The judge was scheduled to rule on the motions the week of July twenty-fifth.

On Sunday night July twenty-fourth, Jerry and I were lying in bed. I couldn't sleep. I was eight months pregnant and there was no position which was comfortable. We began watching the movie, *The Verdict,* in which Paul Newman plays a has-been attorney who makes his comeback representing the family of a woman who suffocated during childbirth and ended up brain-dead.

"Just the type of film I need to see before giving birth myself," I said to Jerry.

Later that night, the contractions started coming. Jerry was convinced it was false labor since it was three weeks early, but, when I felt my water break near 4:00 a.m., I knew this was it.

Jerry grabbed my overnight bag which I had stashed in the corner. By this time Jerry was so nervous he rushed out to the car with it, almost forgetting the one necessity—me. At 3:00 p.m. that afternoon Jack, our first child, was born. Needless to say, the judge granted a continuance in the Bellamy divorce case.

After Jack's birth, I took some time off to enjoy our new son and learn my new mothering tasks. For a while they completely absorbed me. Then one day, viewing *The Incredible Journey*, a story about a dog who, despite huge obstacles, found his way home, I began experiencing a few pangs. Who was taking care of the many wrongs done to animals I'd set out to right?

However, I had a few animal problems of my own: my German shepherd, Dar, had become so depressed by the baby getting all the attention that he had taken up sleeping in a bathroom in the basement. Tucker, the new puppy, saw the baby as a challenge to his being "king" of the dogs. Once again I had to call the animal behaviorists who had assisted me in several cases, but this time it was to assist me with Jack, Dar, and Tucker. They showed me how to teach the dogs that the baby was here to stay and was a part of our family. It was not long before Dar came out of the bathroom and took to sleeping under the baby's crib. He had never been allowed upstairs in our house before, but now he broke all the rules to take over his new role as protector of the baby. Tucker preferred things that way because now he had control of the backyard, the area he had long wanted to dominate. After a few months, the dogs, the baby, Jerry and I settled into our new family situation.

I had not been planning to return to active practice until after the first of the year, but just before Christmas I received a call from Esmeralda and John Bricklande.

"They want to take my babies away," Esmeralda cried.

"Babies!" I echoed, clutching Jack. "But my specialty is dog law."

"My babies are dogs," she said wistfully. "Toy poodles."

I gulped. This I had to see.

"Let me have your address," I said, making an appointment to go and see her.

"Jerry," I called my husband, "would you come with me to see what condition some dogs are in."

"Why?" he questioned, surprised. "I thought you weren't going back till after Christmas?"

"Because they have one hundred four dogs and I need to be sure each one is in good health and well cared for before I defend them."

"A hundred and four?"

"Yeah. Let's just go check it out, please." I added, "And, I'm bringing Jack."

"A hundred and four?" he repeated, not even reacting to my taking our baby on his first dog law case. "That's a new one. You'd better be prepared to count along with me. I'm not sure I trust myself."

I laughed. This case needed at least four good eyes, and two perspectives. Jack's wouldn't hurt either. There just aren't a lot of defenses to owning one hundred and one dogs more than the law permits. I had to see this group for myself before I could represent to the zoning board that owning so many dogs was reasonable.

When we walked into the Briklandes' yellow, chintz-upholstered living room with Jack perched high and comfortable in his pouch strapped on my back, I was amazed how clean and neat the room was. Esmeralda and John invited us to sit down on the comfortable sofa. I looked around. There was no evidence or other sign of any dogs in the house. They offered us Darjeeling tea and tiny scones. We talked about the charges and about the inspection that had been done by animal control officers.

"None of the dogs has been taken away," Mrs. Briklande explained. "I told them that I would be hiring an attorney."

"They said that a state veterinarian would perform a health inspection," Mr. Briklande added, stroking his bald head appraisingly.

As he spoke, I continued to survey the room. There were pictures of children and grandchildren in gold frames on the mantel, an old mahogany television set with a lace doily and a crystal bowl of fruit in the corner, furniture without dog hair. We then asked for a tour of the home. As we walked from room to room, I began to catch on. The dogs were not kept in any one place. They were everywhere, and Jack laughed merrily each time we spied one. There were white poodles in the lazy Susan, one popped up from behind the grandfather clock, three or four lay wrapped together sleeping in a sunny corner, others came out from behind bookshelves and cupboards, and from under furniture. Just about everywhere you looked, there were poodles. All toy, all white. Each of the bedrooms had been converted to dog rooms. The basement was a kennel. The entire home was designed for dogs.

After seeing the house, we were led into the backyard where the younger ones were playing. I stood at the screen door and looked out to a sea of twenty or thirty small white poodles all yapping at me. I started to walk out to see the dogs. What could a few poodles do to me? I wasn't sure, but thirty poodles all biting at my ankles would be like a swarm of bees attacking.

"I think I'll stay inside," I said.

Jerry, who is usually proud of his ability to tame the most vicious of our vicious dog clients, even hesitated. "There's just no good reason to get personal with so many dogs," he said with a straight face. We stayed inside.

But what we had seen at the Briklandes' home was a clean and well-cared-for kennel of poodles. As the investigating animal control officer would later testify, "Some people can't take proper care of one dog, others seem to be able to care for any number of dogs." We had decided this was one of those rare cases where people deserve to keep as many dogs as they could care for, so I took the case. However, I knew that convincing a judge that my client should be able to keep one hundred and four dogs might be a very different thing.

I explained to the Briklandes, "You realize you will have to allow animal control to inspect the property."

"They can inspect to their heart's content, but I want you here, and bring the baby. He's a definite dog lover," Mrs. Briklande, a snappy little lady in her seventies, barked at me.

"That's no problem." I intended to be there, and I had to bring Jack since we'd never had anyone else care for him. "But we will also need your veterinarian there because the state will certainly have their veterinarian examining the dogs. Our own expert opinion is important, in case they discover anything that could be damaging to you."

"Dr. Pike is my veterinarian," Mrs. Briklande informed me. "He'll be here."

I was sure Dr. Pike had to be making a good living caring for the Briklandes' dogs, so I had no doubt he would be available if needed.

We agreed that I would call animal control and schedule the examination for the following day. The next morning we all met back at the Briklande home. Jack sat in my backpack happily surveying the scene. Next to arrive were two animal control officers, the state veterinarian, the zoning inspector, two policemen, and the Briklandes' veterinarian. It was quite a show when you added one hundred and four poodles. Though the inspectors, like mad hatters, ran about the house catching first one poodle then another to examine them I was never sure if they examined all one hundred and four or the same dog a hundred and four times. The examination by both vets was favorable to the Briklandes. The state veterinarian congratulated my clients. "These dogs are all in good health."

Jerry and I looked at each other triumphantly. Jack gurgled at just that moment.

Dr. Pike agreed and the reports were filed with the city attorney's office. Despite the dogs all being in good health, I still had to find some legal grounds for my clients to keep one hundred one dogs more than the zoning ordinance permitted.

The first place to look for a defense to a zoning violation is the local zoning code. I needed to find out how many dogs were permitted in that area, and when was the restriction enacted. What we discovered in the Oodles of Poodles case was that the law restricting dog ownership to only three dogs was a city law. The location of the Briklande home had been outside of the city in an unincorporated part of the county until six years earlier. At that point, because of its growth, the city annexed the area into the city limits. Now the Briklande house fell under the city restrictions on the number of dogs which could be allowed.

"The legal issue," I explained to them, "will hinge on when the law restricting the number of dogs allowed in the city was enacted. If it was after your home was annexed into the city, you won't be protected under any grandfather clause, but, if the law was passed before the area became part of the city, you'll be protected."

Upon further research, I learned that the city restriction had become law three years prior to the annexation. The grandfather clause would apply. Therefore, I argued, the Briklandes should be permitted to make the same use of the property they had been making of it prior to the city annexing their location.

The couple had had at least ninety dogs since the early nineteen sixties, and they had had at least ninety dogs at the time of annexation. They would arguably be entitled to maintain the same use of the property, I reasoned. I was now ready to deal with the city attorney, Brett Holliday, though he didn't realize that when he began teasing me.

Still chuckling to himself, Holliday now asked me, "So, how do you intend to defend these people? Are you going to show the Disney film, since they have one hundred and four poodles in their home?"

"Well, I might," I joked in return. "But, then again, I just might argue that they had at least eighty poodles in their home since the day they bought it in nineteen sixty-one," I responded as Brett looked at me starting to realize where I was coming from.

"Oh yeah," he said, not smiling anymore.

"The Briklandes purchased that home in January of nineteen sixty-one because it was a good place to live along with their eighty or so poodles," I continued. "They checked with zoning and the County of Haraldson and learned that there were no restrictions on the number of dogs they could maintain at that location, so they bought the home."

"So you're going to try the old grandfather tactic," he mused.

"Yes, that old thing which still holds," I said, showing him the law which provided a grandfather provision. "See here," I pointed out, "it provides that whatever use a resident made of the property prior to the enactment of any changes may be continued so long as the use has been continuous. When the Briklandes bought the house they had eighty-eight dogs; therefore, they are entitled to keep eighty-eight dogs."

He frowned, quiet for a time, and then his eyes lighted up. "But that still leaves them with sixteen dogs too many."

I laughed. "I guess that's a minor problem for a woman with one hundred and four dogs."

He was just stalling for time to think of a reason why my argument wouldn't succeed, and we both knew it.

"Now, Brett," I said in a conciliatory tone, "Mrs. Briklande is willing to place sixteen of her dogs." I knew that many of the dogs were puppies and retired show dogs which Mrs. Briklande intended to place in other homes soon anyhow.

He nodded. Silence filled the room. We both knew I had him.

"Here's what I will do," Holliday leaned forward. "Your client will reduce the number of dogs to no more than eighty-eight. She will permit the state veterinarian to examine the dogs and the property to be sure it complies with the state requirements for a kennel. She will obtain a breeder permit from the county and maintain the property accordingly and, as long as there are no violations within one year, the charges will be dropped."

I thought through his offer quickly: although in essence it would be satisfactory to my client because she would be permitted to keep her dogs, the possibility that random inspection by a veterinarian would result in the loss of her dogs if some unsatisfactory condition turned up was too risky. My client wasn't legally required to offer random inspections to the state veterinarian and I couldn't allow her to be that vulnerable. The veterinarian could report some minor uncleanliness at some off-hour, and all of my client's rights to keep her dogs would be lost. I knew the city attorney was setting her up for failure.

"No." I shook my head. "She is not required to have a breeders permit or a kennel license. She is by definition a "hobby breeder" since she does not profit from the sale of her dogs. She is therefore exempt from the breeder permit requirement. Since only state-licensed kennels are required to allow random inspections, she will not obtain a kennel license. Because a kennel license is not permitted in the city limits, she wouldn't be able to obtain one anyhow."

"We'll allow her to get one anyway," Holliday offered, searching for an opening to limit my client's use of the property.

"No thanks," I said, beginning to walk away. "We'll leave things the way they are."

Since Holliday knew that this meant we would be taking the case to trial, it was a good way to test how strongly he felt they could succeed with the charges.

"Hold up a minute," he said, hurrying to my side. "Let me take a look at the law and I'll review your defense with Zoning," Holliday told me. I knew this meant he wanted to delay, hoping he could either think of a reason my defense wouldn't work or a different charge to file against my client to avoid the grandfather clause. I didn't want to delay but I thought I had a strong defense, and we'd made good progress. I didn't want to hurt our chances, so I agreed.

"Let's set a meeting for next Friday," Holliday told me, looking at his calendar. "How's one o'clock?"

I checked my calendar and said, "I'm free."

However, the next day I received a call from Mr. Holliday.

"Linda, Brett Holliday here," he began. "I think we have an offer for your poodle lady that you can live with."

I was curious about what Holliday had learned from Zoning, which made him not want to take the case any further, but I knew he wouldn't tell me, so I didn't ask.

"We'll go ahead and drop the charges," he said, "if your client will agree to reduce her dogs down to eighty-eight. So long as she complies with state regulations on the care of her dogs, we'll leave her alone." I knew this was what I always referred to as a "non-request"—the prosecutor asks for something in return for dropping the charges so it doesn't look like they never should have charged the people in the first place. But we would be giving up nothing in exchange because everyone always has to comply with state regulations anyhow.

"That sounds fine," I said, keeping my voice level, trying not to insinuate that I'd one-upped him. "Just send me the paperwork and we'll accept the plea."

I called Esmeralda and John and told them the good news.

"Gosh golly, thank goodness that hogwash is over," she said.

In her homespun way, she'd read my mind.

Epilogue

When I began dog law in 1988, I had no idea where it would lead me. No one else had ever practiced this specialty. There were very few dog laws, and breeders and owners had little recourse. Now I receive calls from all over this country as well as from Europe from people who have encountered difficulties because of their dogs. I have consulted with many different groups across the world on new laws such as breed bans and breeding regulations. Society and dog owners are more aware of the role of the dog in society and the laws necessary to make animal rights a reality.

The most frustrating and heartbreaking of laws for all dog owners is the law that deems a dog personal property. This is the reason very little can be recovered for the wrongful death of a dog. This is also the basis for people getting away with committing acts of horrific cruelty or gross negligence against dogs resulting in injuries or death. Although judges have been sympathetic to the harsh results of the law, very few have gone so far as to change the laws with their rulings. The only way to change the laws is for dog owners to continue to challenge them, both judicially and legislatively. Dogs are more than personal property, and emotional attachments to pets should be encouraged not punished by our legal system.

If the court system won't work for a dog law case because it is too slow or there is no law available, often the media can be the best forum to try to resolve the dispute. Press coverage has helped aggrieved owners who couldn't sue for the wrongful death of their dogs because of governmental immunity or failure of available laws, gain justice with all legal cases, television has changed the way people look at dogs and the law. I was asked to consult in a case that was tried on television: the O.J. Simpson trial. As I told E Entertainment Network's host, Kathleen Sullivan, "The best witness in the case is the dog, Kato." A dog's temperament can be tested by an animal behaviorist immediately after a traumatic event with some amazing results. If Kato had been properly tested, it could be determined whether the attacker of his mistress had been someone he feared, was submissive to, someone he could have dominated, or someone he didn't know. The tone and nature of the barking could indicate the reaction of the dog to what he had witnessed. The reaction of his estranged wife's dog to O.J. Simpson at the murder site would have, in my opinion, been quite revealing. Unfortunately, no one seriously considered calling Kato the dog as a witness.

Public sympathy to animal rights and new laws regulating how pet owners care for their pets have made owners more responsible. Also, to accommodate the good of the public, often pets must be neutered or spayed, licensed and leashed. To encourage neighborhood harmony, most areas have laws against barking dogs. All of these laws help to make the dog more accepted as a member of society. No longer do dogs roam the streets as they did in the nineteen sixties, but, in those days, there were no doggy day camps for dogs of two working "parents." Today in our pet-loving society of the fast-paced nineties, there are dog overnight camps, day camps, obedience clubs, hotels for dogs, and other amenities to cater to the pet and his or her owner.

Responsibility to a pet is paramount. The owner invests emotionally in his pet, and he or she is therefore responsible for that animal's enjoyment of life and safety. Many groups pursue the rescue of dogs to prevent the needless destruction of so many abandoned dogs. But the law imposes such great liability on these groups that it is usually difficult for them to proceed. But they continue their mission anyway in the best interest of neglected, abandoned, and abused pets.

Today dog law has become recognized worldwide. More lawyers are willing to accept dog-related cases and more owners realize that, as pet owners, they have rights. Judges are not so quick to throw dog cases out of court, although many are still reluctant to hear cases. Slowly, the laws and courts are changing to benefit those like me who love animals and feel their rights should be protected.

For Jack, Jerry and, especially for me, our life is a dream come true. Each time the office telephone rings we eagerly await the excitement, challenges and rewards of being the first family of dog law professionals, defending human beings' best friend, dogs and their owners, from enemies.